Gennaro's
VERDURE

OVER 80 VIBRANT ITALIAN VEGETABLE DISHES

GENNARO CONTALDO
PHOTOGRAPHY BY DAVID LOFTUS

An imprint of Interlink Publishing Group, Inc.
Northampton, Massachusetts

CONTENTS

INTRODUCTION	4

GREEN VEGETABLES

Artichokes	8
Asparagus	16
Fava Beans	24
Broccoli	30
Cabbage	36
Celery	42
Zucchinis	50
Fennel	62
Green Beans	68
Leeks	74
Peas	78
Arugula	86
Salad Greens	92
Spinach	100

RED VEGETABLES

Peppers	108
Swiss Chard	118
Tomatoes	128

SUNSHINE-COLORED VEGETABLES

Belgian Endives	140
Carrots	144
Cauliflower	152
Mushrooms	158
Onions	166
Potatoes	172
Pumpkin/Squash	184

PURPLE VEGETABLES

Eggplants	196
Beets	206
Radicchio	212
Red Cabbage	218

Index	220
Acknowledgments	223

INTRODUCTION

There is so much more to vegetables than a few bland boiled offerings served on the side. In Italy, no one serves plain boiled veggies—they are always flavored or made into something more substantial. Even vegetables that form part of *bollito* (boiled beef or chicken) are served with a drizzle of olive oil and perhaps some wine vinegar to lift the flavor.

Italy is blessed with an incredible diversity of landscape and climate and the breadth of contrast between the cooler northern alpine regions and the warm Mediterranean shores of the south has ensured ideal growing conditions for a wealth of vegetables. Years of foreign invasions and the influence of bordering countries have also introduced an array of wonderful produce. All these have shaped Italy's rich *cucina povera* tradition, where the little that was available was transformed into incredible dishes.

Vegetables were, of course, essential to *cucina povera* as they were often homegrown or easily and cheaply obtainable and consumed in place of expensive meat. In fact, Neapolitans, in the 1900s, were often referred to as *mangia foglie,* which translates as "leaf eaters," for the quantity of vegetables they consumed. However, wonderful vegetable dishes were born out of this necessity and are still enjoyed today.

When I was growing up in Italy, meat was usually only served on Sunday and we had fresh fish on Friday, so vegetables played a very big role in our diet. And this is still more or less true today. When I see a head of broccoli or an eggplant in the fridge, I see meal possibilities. It's amazing what you can create with such humble ingredients; a broccoli head can easily be turned into a baked pasta dish for four or blended into a soup; eggplants can be stuffed or made into the classic *Parmigiana*. You really don't need much to create tasty vegetable dishes and, as long as you have a few basic ingredients in your pantry and fridge, effortless and nutritious meals can be rustled up in no time.

Although most vegetables are available all year round, I am a great believer in buying produce when it is in season. It will be fresher, cheaper, and more sustainable, and it will taste better. In my childhood, the seasons dictated what we ate, and I looked forward to each season for the different produce that it would bring. In fall, we enjoyed earthy wild mushrooms, squash, and beets.

Spring brought all the wonderful herbs, young salad greens, spinach, and asparagus. Summer was a colorful feast for the senses with eggplants, peppers, and tomatoes. Even winter brought joy with broccoli, cauliflower, and root vegetables, alongside all the produce we had so lovingly preserved during the summer.

Although this book is all about vegetables, it is not solely a vegetarian book as, following in the *cucina povera* tradition, I do add a little meat, for example pancetta, Parmesan, or maybe anchovies to quite a few dishes. However, most of these can be omitted, if you prefer, and I include suggestions for each recipe so they can be adapted and made 100 percent vegetarian.

If you are ever in Italy, do pay a visit to the markets where local, seasonal produce is always plentiful. It provides a spectacular sight of wonderful colors, where you can almost taste the season. Cooking with all this fresh produce helps to maintain a healthy, nutrient-rich diet, and I hope that the ideas and recipes in this book will give you lots of inspiration for how to make good use of vegetables and turn them into the superheroes of your meals.

Enjoy and Buon Appetito xx

Artichokes
Asparagus
Fava Beans
Broccoli
Cabbage
Celery
Zucchinis
Fennel
Green Beans
Leeks
Peas
Arugula
Salad Greens
Spinach

GREEN VEGETABLES

ARTICHOKES
CARCIOFI

Although commonly thought of as a vegetable, an artichoke is, in fact, a variety of thistle—it is the young bud of the flower, harvested early, that is consumed. If left to fully develop, the bud turns into a large purple flower, which is no longer edible but rather beautiful to look at.

Artichokes are said to be one of the oldest vegetables around. Historians believe they were first cultivated in North Africa around AD 800 and brought to mainland Italy via Sicily by the Saracens. There is evidence that they were popular amongst the ancient Greeks and Romans, so quickly spread across Europe, and now they are integral to Mediterranean cooking. Italians adore artichokes and are masters at preparing them in a variety of ways. In the 1970s and 80s, an artichoke-based apéritif called Cynar was very popular in Italy, and I believe it is having a comeback today. There is, of course, a Cynar Negroni!

Artichokes thrive in a hot, dry climate and the largest areas of production in Italy are Lazio, Campania, Puglia, and Sicily. Artichoke season starts around the end of October and lasts until the end of spring. There are two main varieties: The *Romanesco* variety is the large purple globe artichoke, while *Violetto Toscano* is also purple but slightly smaller and more pointed in shape. Regional varieties are also produced in smaller quantities all over the country, especially in Veneto and Sardinia.

In Italian markets, artichokes can often be seen piled high in bunches, as well as prepared and ready for the kitchen. In fact, it is not uncommon to see stallholders artfully removing thorny leaves and hairy chokes in a matter of seconds—before dropping them into buckets of acidulated water.

There are numerous ways of cooking artichokes, for example, braising, grilling, blending into soups, and all are delicious. My favorite way to cook them is to stuff them with the flavors of the Mediterranean, or whatever I find in the kitchen. And I also like to preserve or fill the delicate hearts (see page 11) and use the smaller, more tender artichokes for eating raw in salads. Simply dressed with extra virgin olive oil, lemon, and perhaps some Parmesan shavings, they also make a wonderful topping on carpaccio.

In Rome, *Carciofi alla Giudia* (deep-fried and crispy artichokes) is a traditional Jewish recipe and a speciality of the restaurants in Rome's Jewish quarter, where the dish is served every spring. *Carciofi alla Romana* (braised stuffed artichokes with a mixture of garlic, parsley, and mint) is another very popular and typical dish of Roman cuisine.

How to use *artichokes*:

Buying and storing
Look for firmness and tightly packed leaves. Avoid any with brown tips as it means the artichoke is no longer fresh. If possible, buy them still attached to their stems as these will keep fresher for longer, plus you can peel and cook the stems, too. Try to use artichokes as soon as you have bought them. Alternatively, once home, place the artichoke stems in a vase of water as you would flowers. If the artichokes don't have stems, store them in the fridge for up to 2 days.

These days, you can often buy ready-prepared artichoke hearts—either frozen or in cans with brine, as well as the preserved ones in jars that are so delicious in an antipasto. The frozen and canned varieties are a revelation as you can skip the laborious task of cleaning them and use them immediately in your dishes.

Preparing
Fill a bowl or pan with cold water and squeeze in the juice of a whole lemon, plus the squeezed halves. With a small, sharp knife, cut off the artichoke stalk and remove the tougher outer leaves at the base.

With your fingers, gently open it up until you can see the hairy choke. This is the part that would have bloomed into a flower. Remove it with a small scoop or teaspoon and discard.

If you want to use just the hearts, remove all the leaves and extract the hairy choke as above. While preparing the artichokes, place the clean ones in the bowl of lemon water to prevent discoloration.

Cooking
Boil whole artichokes in salted water or, for extra flavor, in vegetable stock. Depending on their size, they will take about 40 minutes. To check they are ready, remove a leaf near the middle and if it pulls away easily, it is done.
Braise—Cut the artichokes into quarters. Sweat extra virgin olive oil and garlic, then stir in the artichokes, cover with salted water or vegetable stock and cook with a lid on for about 30 minutes.
Roast—Preheat the oven to 400°F (200°C). Cut the artichokes into halves or quarters, place in a roasting pan, drizzle with extra virgin olive oil, sprinkle with salt, add squashed garlic cloves, and roast for about 30 minutes.

Eating
The best way to eat them is to tear off a leaf with your fingers and pull off the fleshy base between your teeth, disgarding the hard part of the leaves. Continue eating in this way until you get to the tender heart, which you eat whole. The soothing broth in which the artichokes are cooked is delicious served hot, or you could save it for another time and use it to cook pastina (small pasta shapes), which deliciously absorb the flavor.

FONDO DI CARCIOFI AL TONNO
Tuna-filled *artichoke* hearts

These delicious filled artichoke hearts take a little time to prepare, especially if you are using small artichokes, but they are so worth it. Remember to place the artichokes in acidulated water as you are working (or they will turn black) and reserve the leaves. Here, the leaves are stir-fried and served with the hearts, so nothing is wasted.

SERVES 4

16 small artichokes or 8 globe artichokes
juice of 1 lemon
3 tbsp butter, plus extra for greasing and dotting
⅓ cup (40 g) all-purpose flour
1¾ cups (400 ml) milk
3½ oz (100 g) canned tuna, drained
4 tsp capers
4 tsp finely chopped flat-leaf parsley
dried breadcrumbs, for sprinkling
3 tbsp extra virgin olive oil
2 garlic cloves, left whole and squashed
sea salt and freshly ground black pepper

Clean the artichokes, remove the stems and the leaves until you get to the hearts, then remove and discard the hairy chokes. As you are working, place the hearts and leaves in a bowl of acidulated water from the juice of 1 lemon, or they will turn black.

Bring a large pot of salted water to a boil and cook the hearts and leaves for 10 minutes or until tender. Drain well, placing on a kitchen towel to dry out.

Preheat the oven to 400°F (200°C).

Melt the butter in a pan, then remove from the heat and whisk in the flour until you have a smooth paste. Gradually whisk in the milk, then place back on the heat and continue whisking until you obtain a smooth, creamy consistency. Remove from the heat and, when cool, stir in the tuna, capers, and parsley, and a little salt and pepper to taste.

Lightly grease a large enough baking dish with butter.

Fill the artichoke hearts with the tuna mixture, place in the prepared dish, sprinkle with breadcrumbs, dot with butter, and bake in the oven for 20 minutes until golden.

In the meantime, heat the olive oil in a frying pan, sweat the garlic, add the artichoke leaves, and stir-fry over high heat for about 3 minutes until golden. Remove from the heat and serve immediately with the filled artichoke hearts.

TIP
If you can't find fresh artichokes or don't have the time to clean them, you can use frozen artichoke hearts.

CARCIOFI RIPIENI AL FORNO
Baked filled *artichokes*

Stuffed with leftover bread and a few pantry ingredients, these filled artichokes, served with potatoes, make a deliciously different kind of meal when artichokes are in season.

SERVES 4

4 medium-sized artichokes
juice of 1 lemon
3½ oz (100 g) stale rustic bread, finely chopped
2 small garlic cloves, finely chopped
2 tsp finely chopped flat-leaf parsley
2 eggs
6 tbsp grated Parmesan
breadcrumbs
2 medium-sized potatoes, cut into chunks
generous ½ cup (140 ml) warm water
approx. 2 tbsp extra virgin olive oil
sea salt and freshly ground black pepper

Preheat the oven to 425°F (220°C).

Clean the artichokes, remove the stems and tough outer leaves at the base, then then gently open up the leaves until you get to the center and remove the hairy choke. As you are working, place the artichokes in a bowl of acidulated water using the juice of 1 lemon, or they will turn black.

Bring a large pot of salted water to a boil and cook the hearts and leaves for about 10 minutes until tender. Drain well, placing on a clean kitchen towel to dry out.

In a large bowl, combine the bread, garlic, parsley, eggs, Parmesan, and some salt and pepper to taste, then fill the artichokes with this mixture.

Lightly grease a deep baking dish (a wide loaf pan is ideal) and lightly sprinkle with breadcrumbs. Place the filled artichokes in the dish and arrange the potato chunks around the artichokes—these will help to keep the artichokes upright during cooking. Lightly sprinkle breadcrumbs on top of the artichokes. Carefully pour the water into the dish (about two fingers' depth), drizzle all over with olive oil and cover with foil, then bake in the oven for 1 hour. Serve immediately.

CREMA DI CARCIOFI
Artichoke pâté

It's amazing how far a couple of artichokes will go when you purée them. This delicious and simple pâté, suitable for vegans, is sufficient to top four good slices of rustic toasted bread or to coat 11 oz (320 g) of pasta (dry weight). You can make it in advance, store in the fridge for up to 3 days, and use when required.

SERVES 4

9 oz (250 g) artichokes (about 2 medium-sized)
juice of ½ lemon, plus a few extra drops of lemon juice
2 tbsp extra virgin olive oil
1 tsp capers
½ handful of flat-leaf parsley, roughly chopped
sea salt and freshly ground black pepper

Clean the artichokes, remove the stems and outer leaves, then cut into quarters and remove and discard the hairy choke. As you are working, place the hearts and leaves in a bowl of acidulated water using the juice of half a lemon, or they will turn black.

Bring a large pot of salted water to a boil and cook the artichokes for 20–25 minutes, until cooked through.

Drain well, then transfer the artichokes to a blender with the olive oil, capers, parsley, a few drops of lemon juice, and a little salt and pepper to taste. Blend to a smooth purée.

Spread the pâté on crostini or toss through freshly cooked pasta, such as *manfreddine* (curly tagliatelle), linguine, spaghetti, or penne.

ASPARAGUS

What we call asparagus is the young, tender shoot of a plant (*Asparagus officinalis*) that, if allowed to grow to maturity, would turn woody at the base and the spears blossom into pretty, fern-like foliage. It is an ancient vegetable and its name derives from the Greek *aspharagos,* and Latin *asparagus,* meaning to "shoot," or "spring up." It was very popular during Roman times, when it was used for culinary and medicinal purposes and seen as an aphrodisiac.

Asparagus can be wild or cultivated. The spears of the wild variety tend to be much thinner, and I remember as a child in Italy picking them during springtime walks in the countryside. In fact, wild asparagus grows all over Italy in rural areas and foraging for it is quite a popular pastime as the days become warmer. The season is relatively short (from about March until June) but it is always a treat, and the best time to eat asparagus is when it is fresh, local, and in abundance.

In Italy, three types of asparagus are cultivated—green, white, and a pretty purple-tipped variety. White asparagus is specially grown underground without sunlight and is white because it lacks chlorophyll. Mainly cultivated in the northern Po Valley, asparagus connoisseurs rate this white variety very highly for its flavor, and especially the most sought-after *Bianco di Bassano* variety, which is grown in the Veneto region. The story goes that it was discovered by accident in the sixteenth century. A violent hailstorm almost ruined every asparagus farmer's crop, until they discovered that the white part in the ground actually tasted really good. Since then, white asparagus has been a delicacy and the Veneto region prides itself on the various *sagre* (food festivals) that celebrate this highly prized vegetable.

The pretty, purple-tipped asparagus is grown in Albenga near the Ligurian coast. The unusual color comes from its genetic heritage and not cultivation techniques. Known as *Violetto d'Albenga*, it tends to be sweeter in taste and more tender than other asparagus varieties and is ideal eaten raw in salads. Sadly, it is not cultivated in large quantities, but the Slow Food Society is trying to encourage its revival. The popular green variety is mainly grown in northern Italy, especially in Emilia Romagna, but it is a very popular vegetable throughout the country and Italy is one of the biggest producers in Europe.

From appetizers to main course dishes, Italians love to use asparagus as much as they can during the season. The simplest way to prepare it is to boil or steam it, then dress it with some extra virgin olive oil and a squeeze of lemon juice. I love to serve the small, thin asparagus tips raw in a salad, and adding a poached egg on top with shavings of Parmesan makes a popular Milanese main course. In fact, asparagus goes perfectly with eggs, Parmesan, pancetta, prosciutto, melted butter, and balsamic vinegar, to name a few ingredients. It is especially good with a classic *Carbonara* (see page 23), and I frequently chop it finely and add to pasta, risotto, frittata, and savory tarts (see page 20).

As well as being incredibly delicious, asparagus also contains very few calories, is packed with vitamins and minerals, and is said to help with digestion as well as lower blood pressure. Therefore, when in season, I urge you to enjoy it in as many ways as possible. The recipes that follow all use the easily obtainable green variety of asparagus.

How to use *asparagus*:

Buying and storing
Look for straight, bright green stalks with smooth skin and tightly closed tips that are firm to the touch. Avoid any that look dry or wrinkled. Once home, they are best cooked the same day, but can be kept in the fridge for a couple of days. If you want to preserve their freshness, trim the hard stems, place in a jar with a little water, and keep in the fridge.

Preparing
First remove the hard stem at the bottom of the spears, which tends to be tough and fibrous. If necessary, use a potato peeler to remove the slightly rough outer skin from just under the spear tip to the base. However, if the outer skin does not feel tough, don't bother. Thin spears, especially the ones you buy pre-packaged in supermarkets, tend to be ready and don't need to be trimmed or pared.

Tie the asparagus in a bundle with cooking string, then stand upright in a pot of salted boiling water with the tips sticking out and cook for 3–5 minutes, depending on size, until tender.

Asparagus spears are delicious grilled or broiled, too. Simply brush with a little olive oil and place on a hot grill or under the broiler for about 5 minutes, turning them over frequently to char evenly. Sprinkle with salt and pepper, then drizzle with extra virgin olive oil and either lemon juice or balsamic vinegar before serving.

ASPARAGI ALLA VALDOSTANA
Baked cheesy *asparagus*

This dish comes from the Italian alpine region and makes the most of its local fontina cheese, which has perfect melting properties. It's a simple and nutritious meal for any time but especially in the spring, when asparagus is plentiful. You should be able to find fontina in good Italian delis. However, if not available, a good strong Cheddar makes a great substitute.

SERVES 4

1 lb 2 oz (500 g) asparagus
pats of butter, plus extra for greasing
4¼ oz (120 g) fontina, grated
4 slices of cooked ham
  (approx. 4¼ oz/120 g)
4 eggs
¼ cup (30 g) grated Parmesan
sea salt and freshly ground black pepper

Preheat the oven to 350°F (180°C).

Bring a pot of salted water to a boil. Remove any hard stems from the asparagus, then add to the pot and cook for about 5 minutes until tender but not mushy. Carefully transfer to a kitchen towel to drain and pat dry to remove any excess water.

Lightly grease a baking dish with butter and lay the asparagus spears on top. Dot with a little butter, sprinkle over half of the grated fontina, followed by the slices of ham, and then the remaining fontina.

Lightly beat the eggs with some salt and pepper, then pour this over and sprinkle with Parmesan. Bake in the oven for 15 minutes, until the egg has cooked and the top is golden.

TORTA SALATA DI ASPARAGI
Savory *asparagus* tart

This delicious savory tart is made for the spring, when asparagus is plentiful and at its best. If you don't have prosciutto, use cooked ham or, if you don't eat meat, omit altogether. Serve with a crunchy mixed salad.

SERVES 4

13 oz (375 g) ready-made shortcrust pastry, thawed if frozen
7 oz (200 g) asparagus
⅔ cup (150 g) ricotta
4 eggs
¼ cup (30 g) grated Parmesan
3½ oz (100 g) prosciutto, roughly torn
sea salt and freshly ground black pepper
crunchy mixed salad, to serve

Preheat the oven to 400°F (200°C). Grease an 8½ in (22 cm) round tart or quiche pan and line it with parchment paper.

Roll out the pastry and use it to line the bottom of the prepared pan. Cover the pastry with parchment paper, top with pie weights, and blind bake for about 15 minutes, until the sides of the pastry have cooked through and are golden.

Using a large spoon, remove the weights and then the parchment paper from the pastry crust and return the pastry to the oven for a further 5–10 minutes, until the crust is a pale golden color. Remove from the oven and prepare the filling.

Reduce the oven temperature to 300°F (150°C).

Finely chop most of the asparagus, reserving 7 or 8 spears, then bring a pot of salted water to a boil and cook the asparagus for about 3 minutes until just tender, then drain well and leave to cool.

In a bowl, combine the ricotta, eggs, Parmesan, prosciutto, a little salt and pepper, and the chopped asparagus. Fill the pastry crust with this mixture, then arrange the whole asparagus spears over the top. Bake in the lower third of the oven for about 40 minutes, until the filling has set.

Remove from the oven and leave to rest for 5 minutes before serving with a potato salad.

CARBONARA DI ASPARAGI
Pasta with *asparagus* carbonara

A classic *Carbonara* is loved the world over and the addition of asparagus brings a lovely fresh flavor. I even use the hard stems to flavor the pasta water. Vegetarians can simply omit the pancetta and use a vegetarian pecorino-style cheese. And don't throw out the egg whites; store them in the fridge and use them the next day to make a lovely light omelet.

SERVES 4

11 oz (320 g) asparagus
11 oz (320 g) linguine pasta
3 tbsp extra virgin olive oil
2 oz (60 g) pancetta, finely chopped
6 egg yolks
¾ cup (80 g) grated pecorino cheese, plus extra for sprinkling
sea salt and freshly ground black pepper

Remove any hard stems from the asparagus, then finely chop the remaining stems and keep the asparagus tips intact. Set aside.

Bring a pot of salted water to a boil and add the woody asparagus stems. When the water begins to boil, discard the asparagus, add the linguine pasta, and cook until al dente.

Meanwhile, heat the olive oil in a large frying pan over medium heat, add the pancetta, and sweat for 2–3 minutes until it begins to color. Stir in the finely chopped asparagus stems and tips and stir-fry for about 3 minutes until the asparagus is cooked.

In a bowl, lightly beat the egg yolks, then stir through a little black pepper and the pecorino.

Drain the cooked linguine, reserving some of the pasta water, and add to the frying pan with the asparagus. Mix well together, adding a little of the hot pasta water to bind. Remove from the heat and quickly stir in the egg-yolk mixture, until everything is well combined and silky.

Serve immediately with a sprinkling of black pepper and extra grated pecorino, if desired.

FAVA BEANS
FAVE

Each spring, Italians eagerly await the arrival of fresh fava beans, when grocery stores and markets come alive with the new season's produce and stalls are piled high with pods. The season is very short, so Italians really make the most of the fresh variety in all sorts of ways, even enjoying them raw.

Known as *fave* in Italian and from the *Fabaceae* family, fava beans are an easy crop to grow as they thrive in cool and temperate climates. They have a long history of cultivation and although their origins are unclear, they were popular among the ancient Greeks and Romans.

Fava beans are steeped in tradition and often seen as a symbol of good luck. The Romans even saw them as a means to communicate with the dead. In fact, fava bean seeds are traditionally sown at the beginning of November, specifically on the day of All Souls, and cookies known as *Fave dei Morti*, formed in the shape of fava beans, are made to celebrate this feast.

In Rome and the surrounding areas, the tradition on the first May holiday weekend is to picnic and enjoy fresh fava beans with local pecorino cheese. This dates back to ancient times when fava beans were seen as a symbol of fertility and rebirth and offered up to Flora, the Roman goddess of spring, nature, and flowers, and my recipe for *Spaghetti con Fave e Pecorino* on page 27 is a nod to this springtime ritual. A little earlier in the year, on St. Joseph's day in March, *Maccu e Pasta* (puréed dried fava beans and pasta) is a traditional dish served in Sicily on this feast day.

Italians have always loved fava beans and they are used in many recipes from the *cucina povera* tradition as a meat substitute. The fava bean has excellent nutritional properties with high levels of carbohydrates and protein, so it is no wonder that it was highly prized in poor, rural communities. *Fave e Cicoria*, a traditional recipe from Puglia, consists of mashed beans with locally grown greens, which makes a highly nutritious dish. Also *Macco di Fave*, from Sicily, uses dried fava beans to make a thick purée, seasoned with extra virgin olive oil and salt and pepper, and is still popular today. My recipe for *Favata* on page 26 is a split fava bean stew and also comes from this rich culinary tradition.

Fresh fava beans have a short season, but you can also use them frozen and dried and so can enjoy them all year round. I always like to have both on hand in the kitchen as they can be used in so many dishes—mashed or left whole, in pasta, risotto, soups and stews, or simply braised with olive oil, onion, and pancetta.

How to use fava beans:

Buying and storing
When buying fresh, look for pods that are firm and bright green. The smaller the pods, the fewer beans they will contain, so you will need to buy a large amount to make a dish. The pods tend to be wasted and yet they are edible and I like to add them to stocks and stews, or even fry them for a snack.

Preparing
Fresh fava beans take a little time to prepare as they require double-podding, first from their thick outer pods and then again from their skins. First, crack open the green pods. Inside the velvety jackets the beans pop out—depending on the size of the pod, you will find 3–6 beans per pod. If the beans are young enough, you can then pop them out of their skin. If not, simply blanch them in boiling water for a couple of minutes and then drain and the skins will come off easily and the bright green bean will pop out. Although it takes a little time, it really is worth the effort to prepare fresh fava beans and is a lovely springtime treat—the freshness really comes out.

Frozen fava beans are, of course, podded, but tend to come with the skins on, so you will need to give them a quick blanch before using them in your recipe.

Dried fava beans come in two varieties. The whole ones, with their skins still on, are brown. The split dried beans are a creamy color and I tend to buy these as they are quicker to cook. Always check the package for cooking instructions, but I find that there is no need to soak the split beans and they cook in about 30 minutes.

Once cooked, the fresh or frozen fava beans have a mild and slightly sweet flavor, but the cooked dried fava beans have, in contrast, a strong earthy, almost smoky flavor. The two are really quite different and you could mistake them for a completely different vegetable.

FAVATA
Split *fava bean* stew

This Sardinian winter warmer comes from the *cucina povera* tradition and uses dried fava beans with bits of pork for extra flavor. I really like the distinct flavor of the dried beans, but you could use fresh or frozen ones. For my version, I'm using ribs and sausages because the original one includes pork rind and other less known pork cuts. Serve with rustic bread or Sardinian *Pane Carasau* for a hearty meal.

SERVES 4

2 tbsp extra virgin olive oil
9¾ oz (275 g) pork ribs
10½ oz (300 g) Italian pork sausages
1 onion, finely sliced
1 fennel bulb, finely sliced
1 tsp fennel seeds
1 tbsp tomato paste, diluted in a little water
2 cups (350 g) dried split fava beans
approx. 2¾ cups (650 ml) vegetable stock
finely chopped flat-leaf parsley and red pepper flakes (optional), to garnish

Heat the olive oil in a large pot over medium heat, add the pork ribs and sausages, and sear well on all sides. Stir in the onion and fennel, cover with a lid, and sweat for 15 minutes. Add the fennel seeds and tomato paste and continue to cook, covered with a lid, for a further 15 minutes.

Add the dried fava beans to the pot together with the vegetable stock, bring to a boil, then cover with a lid and cook over gentle heat for about 40 minutes, until the beans are cooked through.

Remove from the heat and serve with some freshly chopped parsley and red pepper flakes, if you like.

SPAGHETTI CON FAVE E PECORINO
Spaghetti with *fava beans* and pecorino

Fava beans and pecorino cheese are a match made in heaven—in fact, in rural Puglia, farmers often enjoy the first fresh springtime fava beans straight from the pod with a piece of local pecorino cheese. To enable you to make this dish at any time of the year, I opted for frozen fava beans, but of course use fresh, if you can.

SERVES 4

12 oz (350 g) frozen fava beans
¼ cup (60 ml) extra virgin olive oil
2 banana shallots, finely chopped
8 mint leaves, finely chopped
11 oz (320 g) spaghetti
½ cup (60 g) grated pecorino cheese, plus extra for sprinkling
sea salt and freshly ground black pepper

Bring a pot of salted water to a boil and blanch the fava beans for a minute or so—this is to soften the skins. Drain and remove the skins.

Heat the olive oil in a large frying pan over medium heat and sweat the shallots until softened. Add the skinless fava beans, a little salt, the mint, and 2 ladles of hot water. Reduce the heat and leave to cook for 12–15 minutes, until the fava beans are tender and you obtain a creamy consistency.

In the meantime, bring another pot of salted water to a boil and cook the spaghetti until al dente.

Transfer the cooked spaghetti with a little of the pasta water to the fava beans and place over medium-high heat. Add the pecorino and stir well for a minute or so until everything is nicely combined and creamy.

Remove from the heat and serve immediately with an extra sprinkling of grated pecorino and a twist of black pepper.

TIP
If using fresh fava beans, you will need the same quantity as frozen, ready-podded. There is no need to blanch them; simply removing the skins on either frozen or fresh, will bring a lovely creaminess to the dish.

Green Vegetables

FRITTEDDA SICILIANA
Artichokes with peas and *fava beans*

This Sicilian dish, with fresh peas and fava beans, represents "spring on a plate." However, I like to make it at any time of the year, using frozen peas and beans and canned artichokes. The combination of vinegar and sugar gives the vegetables a lovely tangy flavor, which works so well with the freshness of the mint. You can serve it as a warm or cold salad, with lots of rustic bread, but do make a little in advance—ideally the day before—as this allows the flavors to really come out.

SERVES 4–6

6 medium-sized artichokes
juice of 1 lemon
¼ cup (60 ml) extra virgin olive oil
1 onion, finely chopped
2½ cups (600 ml) vegetable stock
14 oz (400 g) frozen peas
1 lb 2 oz (500 g) frozen fava beans
8 mint leaves, finely chopped, plus extra whole sprigs to garnish
2 tbsp white wine vinegar
2 tsp sugar (whatever type you have on hand)

Clean the artichokes, remove the hairy chokes, cut into quarters, and place in a bowl of acidulated water (using the juice of 1 lemon).

Heat the olive oil in a pot over medium heat and sweat the onion for a couple of minutes. Drain the artichokes, pat them dry, then add them to the pot and stir-fry for a couple of minutes.

Add the stock, cover with a lid, and cook over medium-low heat for 5 minutes. Add the peas and fava beans, cover, and continue to cook for about 10 minutes until all the vegetables are cooked. Stir in the chopped mint, vinegar, and sugar and cook for a couple of minutes.

Remove from the heat, leave to rest for 5 minutes, then garnish with some sprigs of fresh mint and serve.

BROCCOLI

The word "broccoli" is Italian and it's no wonder, as this vegetable's origins date back to early Roman times and Italy, along with Spain, is still one of the largest producers—the main regions of cultivation are Puglia, Campania, Calabria, and Tuscany. Broccoli belongs to the brassica family, which also includes cabbage, cauliflower, and Brussels sprouts. If broccoli is left to grow, the buds open up and turn into brightly colored yellow flowers that, although edible, taste bitter. Therefore growers must ensure broccoli is harvested before this happens.

The most widely used broccoli is the large-headed, bluey-green variety, which is known in Italy as *Calabrese* as it comes from Calabria in the south. Purple sprouting and tenderstem broccoli is known as *broccolini* (small broccoli). It does not come as a large head, like the *Calabrese*, but has small, pretty heads and long, thin, tender stalks. This variety is widely available in Italy from late February and throughout the spring. It's sweet, tender, and prefers gentle cooking.

Italians also love *Broccoli di Rape*, a vegetable that, in spite of its name, isn't in fact a broccoli as it comes from the turnip family and is used in much the same way. It is also known as *rapini*, *broccoletti*, and *cime di rapa*. The shoots and leaves are used to make the popular Puglian pasta dish *Orecchiette con Cime di Rape*, but you can also make it with any other type of broccoli.

Romanesco is another type of broccoli that grows in the cooler north of Italy during winter. A lighter green, almost lime in color, it has a head of what look like pretty little pointy Christmas trees, packed together. It has a nutty flavor and needs cooking for a little longer than broccoli or cauliflower.

Italians enjoy broccoli in many ways but boiling is not so common. It is full of goodness (high in B and C vitamins, fiber, and also a little protein, which is unusual in vegetables) but it does need other flavorings to bring out the taste. Italians often dress broccoli with a little extra virgin olive oil, garlic, and a touch of chile. Otherwise, it combines perfectly with anchovies, garlic, chile, black olives, raisins, and cheeses like pecorino, Parmesan, and fontina. It is excellent blended into a soup (see page 31), or used in various pasta and risotto dishes. I like to turn it into fritters (see page 32) or mash it into a purée, or it is lovely in a frittata or cheesy bake, or simply dressed in a salad.

How to use *broccoli*:

Buying and storing
When buying broccoli, look for firm, brightly colored heads and store in a cool part of the kitchen or in the fridge for a couple of days at the most. Broccoli can deteriorate quite quickly, with the florets turning yellow and the stalks woody.

Preparing
To prepare a broccoli head, break off the florets and use as much of the stalk as you can—if the stalk is a little tough, peel off the outer skin. Chop the stalk into small pieces so it all cooks for the same time. The stalk is delicious, there is no need to waste it.

VELLUTATA DI BROCCOLI CON FORMAGGIO
Cheesy *broccoli* soup

This simple soup wastes almost nothing of a delicious broccoli head and makes the most of its tender stem, which is often discarded. Parmesan rind and freshly grated cheese are added to give it a nice rich cheesy flavor. Serve with rustic bread for a warming, nutritious meal.

SERVES 4

1 broccoli head (approx. 12½ oz/360 g)
3 tbsp extra virgin olive oil
1 leek, finely sliced
1 medium-sized potato, peeled and cut into small chunks
3¾ cups (900 ml) hot vegetable stock
¾ oz (20 g) Parmesan rind, cut into small chunks
3 tbsp (20 g) grated Parmesan
freshly ground black pepper

Break the broccoli up into florets and discard the tough stem but finely chop the tender part. Set aside.

Warm the olive oil in a large pot over medium heat and sweat the leek for a couple of minutes to soften. Add the broccoli florets and finely chopped stem and then stir in the potato chunks. Pour in the hot stock, increase the heat to bring to a boil, then reduce to medium-low and simmer gently for about 20 minutes until the broccoli is cooked through. About halfway through cooking, add the Parmesan rind.

Remove from the heat and blend until smooth. Stir in the grated Parmesan and a little black pepper and heat through gently, if necessary, then serve immediately.

FRITTELLE DI BROCCOLI
Broccoli fritters

Here, broccoli and a few everyday ingredients are transformed into delicious fritters. Quick and simple to prepare, they especially appeal to kids who often refuse to eat their greens! And adults will love them, too. Serve straight away, while still warm, along with a crunchy mixed salad.

MAKES ABOUT 10

1 broccoli head, broken into florets (or 9¾ oz/275 g broccoli florets)
3½ oz (100 g) all-purpose flour, sifted
2 eggs
⅓ cup (80 ml) milk
1 tsp sea salt
1 tsp red pepper flakes (optional)
abundant vegetable or sunflower oil, for frying
6 tbsp grated Parmesan
fresh red chile to finish, deseeded and finely chopped (optional)

Bring a pot of salted water to a boil and cook the broccoli florets for 5–10 minutes until cooked through, then drain well and lightly mash with a fork. Set aside.

In a bowl, combine the flour, eggs, milk, salt, and red pepper flakes (if using) and whisk until you obtain a thick, smooth batter. Stir in the mashed broccoli, mixing well.

Heat plenty of oil in a large, deep frying pan until hot, then drop in a few tablespoons of the broccoli batter (you will need to cook these in batches), flattening them slightly with the back of a spoon or spatula. Cook for 2–3 minutes on each side, until golden all over.

Remove and drain well on paper towels to soak up any excess oil. Keep warm until all the fritters are cooked and then serve immediately. Sprinkle over the Parmesan and top with finely chopped fresh chile, if you like.

BROCCOLI ALLA SICILIANA
Broccoli cooked in red wine with provolone cheese

In this typical Sicilian dish, broccoli is cooked over low heat with cheese, wine, and olives. Local Sicilian cheeses, like *tuma* or *caciocavallo,* are usually used, but I like a strong provolone or a hard pecorino. Once you've prepped your ingredients, it's so easy to make as the pan does all the work. Traditionally served as an appetizer or side dish, it can also make a nutritious main if served with lots of rustic bread.

SERVES 2–4 (2 AS A MAIN OR 4 AS A SIDE)

3 tbsp extra virgin olive oil
1 large onion, finely sliced
3 anchovy fillets, finely chopped
1 broccoli head, broken into florets (or 10 oz/280 g broccoli florets)
25 pitted black olives
1¾ oz (50 g) provolone picante, thinly sliced and chopped
⅔ cup (150 ml) red wine
sea salt
rustic bread, to serve

Heat 1 tablespoon of olive oil in a heavy-based pan over low heat, then add half of the onion, half of the anchovies, half of the broccoli florets, half of the olives, and half of the provolone. Stir together, sprinkle with a little salt, and drizzle with 1 tablespoon of olive oil.

Make another layer with the remaining same ingredients, sprinkling a little salt over the top and drizzling with the remaining olive oil.

Pour over the red wine, reduce the heat, cover with a lid, and leave to cook for about 45 minutes, until the broccoli is tender.

Remove the lid, increase the heat, and allow the majority of the wine to evaporate.

Finish with some grated provolone cheese and serve with rustic bread.

CABBAGE
CAVOLO

Why does the mere mention of cabbage cause noses to wrinkle? Is it memories of bland, overboiled school lunch offerings, or the smell that lingers in hospital hallways? But it shouldn't be this way! When I was growing up in Italy, cabbage was anything but bland. It has always been thought of as "poor man's food," but with a little creativity, it can easily be turned into a delicious vegetable.

Along with broccoli and cauliflower, cabbage is part of the brassica family and has been around for a very long time—probably first encountered in China many thousands of years ago. Wild cabbage grew along the Mediterranean coast and, for the ancient Greeks and Romans, it was highly prized. The Romans cultivated many different varieties, which were used in the kitchen as well as for a wealth of medicinal purposes as it was believed to aid virility and longevity.

The most popular varieties of cabbage grown in Italy today are *Verza, Cappuccia, Rosso,* and *Cavolo Nero*.

Verza or *Savoia*, Savoy cabbage, is predominantly produced in northern Italy and sometimes referred to as *Cavolo di Milano* or *Lombardo*. Available during the fall and winter, this dark green cabbage with large, wrinkled leaves is perfect to stuff whole or to make *involtini*, or for wrapping the leaves around a filling to make small, delicious parcels (see page 38). The leaves can also be finely sliced and simply braised, then dressed with a little extra virgin olive oil and lemon or vinegar. They can also be added to soups, bean stews, or the traditional Milanese pork stew *Cassoeula*. In the mountains of Valtellina, a region in Lombardy, a hearty buckwheat pasta dish (known locally as *Pizzoccheri*) combines Savoy cabbage with potatoes and local cheese and is perfect for keeping you going on cold mountain walks.

Cappuccia, with its pale green exterior leaves and white interior, is grown mainly in the north-east of Italy but enjoyed everywhere. The northern Trentino-Alto Adige region has an Austrian influence and there it is often made into *crauti* (sauerkraut), or slow-cooked with local sausages, or combined with local cheese to fill ravioli. In Sicily, *Cappuccia* is slow-cooked with a little white wine and a touch of tomato paste for color. This type of cabbage, if very finely sliced, is also excellent eaten raw in salads.

Cavolo Nero (lacinato or Tuscan kale) is a loose-leafed cabbage that grows in Tuscany. Its characteristic thick, crinkly leaves are dark green, almost black in color, hence the Italian name *Cavolo Nero,* which translates as "black cabbage." In Italy, it is used in many recipes, namely *Ribollita,* the classic Tuscan bean and bread soup. It can also be added to minestrone and other vegetable soups, as well as pasta dishes, or served with polenta. Simply braised with extra virgin olive oil and garlic, it makes a wonderful side dish or bruschetta topping. For a delicious snack, you can also chop it and either fry it or bake in the oven with olive oil and sea salt until nice and crispy.

How to prepare cabbage:

Buying and storing
Look for crisp, dark green outer leaves. These tend to be tough and are usually discarded. Since the interior leaves are hidden from the sun, the color tends to fade inwards to pale yellow and white. If you are not using the cabbage straight away, store in a cool, dark place in the kitchen for a day or so and leave the outer leaves intact as a way of protecting the interior.

Preparing cavolo nero
Remove the tough stems and use the dark green leaves. Available during summer and fall, it is sold in bundles and, although more expensive than the other cabbage varieties, it is milder in taste and extremely nutritious; packed with vitamins, plus a good source of iron.

FOGLIE DI CAVOLO RIPIENE CON SALSA AL POMODORO
Stuffed *cabbage* leaves in tomato sauce

This nourishing dish comes from northern Italy and is comfort food at its best. I love to serve it with creamy mashed potatoes. It does take a little time to prepare but is so worth it. Reserve the largest cabbage leaves and whatever you have left over to use another time in a soup or stew.

SERVES 4

12 large Savoy cabbage leaves
1 tbsp extra virgin olive oil
½ onion, very finely chopped
1 oz (30 g) pancetta, very finely chopped
½ celery stalk, very finely chopped
½ carrot, very finely chopped
10½ oz (300 g) ground turkey
2 bay leaves
3 sage leaves
whole needles of 1 small rosemary sprig
¾ oz (20 g) stale bread, soaked in a little water to soften
3 tbsp (20 g) grated Parmesan
1 egg
sea salt and freshly ground black pepper

For the tomato sauce
2 tbsp extra virgin olive oil
½ onion, finely chopped
2 x 14 oz (400 g) cans chopped tomatoes
sea salt and freshly ground black pepper

First make the tomato sauce. Heat the oil in a large, heavy-based pot and sweat the onion until softened. Stir in the tomatoes, season with a little salt and pepper, cover with a lid, and gently simmer over medium-low heat for about 15 minutes.

Meanwhile, take each cabbage leaf and, using a small, sharp knife, carefully remove the hard white stalk and discard. Set aside.

Heat the olive oil in another large, heavy-based pot over medium heat and sweat the onion and pancetta for a couple of minutes. Stir in the celery and carrot and continue to sweat for 2 minutes. Add the ground turkey and herbs and some salt and pepper and sear the meat. Remove from the heat and remove the bay leaves. Using a handheld immersion blender, blend until smooth.

Squeeze the bread with your hands to remove the excess water, then add the softened bread to the turkey, together with the Parmesan and egg.

When the mixture is cool enough to handle, divide into 12 and, using your hands, form into oval-shaped *polpettine*. Place one on each cabbage leaf and wrap well, patting down with your hand to secure the filling. Use toothpicks to secure, if necessary.

When all the cabbage leaves are stuffed, carefully place them, one by one, into the tomato sauce, then cover with a lid and cook over medium heat for about 55 minutes. Check from time to time to see if the sauce is drying out and add a little hot water if so.

When the cabbage leaves are tender, serve the stuffed cabbage leaves with the tomato sauce.

MINESTRA DI CAVOLO
Cabbage soup

Cabbage soup was a popular *cucina povera* dish in rural areas when this winter vegetable was in abundance. It still is today and often enriched with other vegetables or pasta to make it go further and provide extra nutrition. You can use any type of green cabbage in this recipe, which is a perfect one-pot winter warmer.

SERVES 4

1½ tbsp extra virgin olive oil
1 onion, finely chopped
1 oz (30 g) pancetta, very finely chopped (optional)
1 garlic clove, finely sliced
½ celery stalk, finely chopped
1 small carrot, finely chopped
1 small sweetheart cabbage (approx. 10 oz/285 g)
4½ oz (125 g) cavolo nero (lacinato kale)
1 tbsp tomato paste, diluted in a little hot water
1 small potato (approx. 3 oz/80 g), peeled and cut into small chunks
5¼ cups (1.25 liters) hot vegetable stock
5 oz (140 g) tagliatelle, broken up
freshly ground black pepper

Heat the olive oil in a large pot over medium heat and sweat the onion, pancetta (if using), garlic, celery, and carrot for about 5 minutes, until the pancetta fat (if using) renders nicely and the vegetables soften.

Meanwhile, discard the hard interior core of the sweetheart cabbage and roughly chop the leaves. Also remove the hard central stem of the cavolo nero and discard, then roughly chop the dark green leaves.

Stir the diluted tomato paste into the *soffritto* (the cooked vegetables), followed by the chopped cabbages and potato and cook for a couple of minutes. Pour in the stock, cover with a lid, and cook gently for about 1 hour, until the cabbage is cooked through.

Increase the heat, add the pasta, and stir to combine, then cook for about 10 minutes, until the pasta is al dente.

Remove from the heat and serve immediately with a sprinkling of black pepper.

STRUDEL DI VERZA CON RICOTTA AL FORNO
Cabbage strudel with baked ricotta

This simple strudel or pie is a fabulous way of making the humble cabbage go further. I use Savoy, but you could use sweetheart or pointed cabbage, green cabbage, or a bag of mixed greens. Baking the ricotta makes it firmer so you can actually see the chunks of cheese when you slice up the cooked pie. If you prefer, you can substitute with feta. For vegetarians, simply omit the ham and Parmesan by adding more ricotta. Serve with a boiled new potato salad for a delicious, comforting meal.

SERVES 4

1 Savoy cabbage (approx. 1 lb 2 oz/ 500 g) cut into thin strips
2 tbsp extra virgin olive oil
1 onion, finely chopped
$2/3$ cup (150 g) ricotta
5½ oz (150 g) cooked ham, finely chopped
3 tbsp grated Parmesan
1 x 11 oz (320 g) sheet of ready-rolled shortcrust pastry, thawed if frozen
sea salt and freshly ground black pepper

Preheat the oven to 400°F (200°C).

Bring a pot of salted water to a boil and cook the cabbage for 5 minutes, then drain.

Heat the olive oil in a large frying pan over medium heat and sweat the onion for 3 minutes. Add the drained cabbage, stir to combine, then cover with a lid and cook for 25–30 minutes, until the cabbage is cooked through.

Meanwhile, drain the ricotta of any excess liquid, place in a small baking dish, and bake in the oven for about 20 minutes, until it has dried out and is just starting to color.

When the cabbage is cooked, remove from the heat, stir in the cooked ham and Parmesan, and crumble in the baked ricotta. Season to taste. Set aside to cool.

Unroll the prepared pastry sheet and place it on a baking sheet lined with parchment paper. Spread the cabbage filling all over, then carefully roll up the pastry from a longer side, securing the ends well. Seal and tuck so the filling does not escape, like you would when making an apple strudel.

Bake in the oven for about 20 minutes until golden, then rest for about 5 minutes, slice, and serve.

Green Vegetables

CELERY
SEDANO

Although a somewhat underappreciated vegetable elsewhere, celery is indispensable in the Italian kitchen. Its distinct, fresh flavor is a must in many dishes and it is, of course, an integral part of the *soffritto* that forms the base of so many sauces, soups, ragùs, risottos, and stews.

Wild celery, known as *smallage*, originated in southern Mediterranean areas as well as China. A member of the parsley family, it was known as *selinous* in Sicily after the wild parsley that grew there. The Ancient Greeks and Romans prized it for its medicinal properties, as well as its ability, supposedly, to ward off the evil eye, and the leaves were often used to adorn wreaths and garlands.

Italians domesticated the plant as a vegetable around the seventeenth century and, over time, it evolved into the celery we know today; less bitter tasting and with solid stalks.

In Italy, the two main types of celery are white and green. The white or blanched variety is usually available during the winter. It has thick stalks, dark green leaves, and a sweet taste. The green variety has thinner stalks with yellow or pale green leaves and a slightly stronger flavor.

There is also a third variety of celery called celeriac (or celery root). Known in Italy as *Sedano Rapa,* meaning turnip celery, it is the bulbous root that is consumed and not the leafy green top. It has a distinctive knobbly appearance and a deliciously sweet, nutty flavor. It is usually boiled and then mashed with carrot or potato, or made into creamy soups or bakes. Sliced very finely or grated, it also makes a lovely addition to winter salads.

Celery is obtainable all year round and I always look for ones with lots of leaves. Unfortunately, the majority of celery leaves are cut off before they reach the stores because they tend to deteriorate quickly and make the stalks limp. This is a shame because there is so much flavor in the leaves and I use them a lot in my cooking. I tend to cut them off, wrap them in damp paper towels, and store in the fridge. They won't last as long as the stalks, but at least this way they can be used for a little bit longer and are delicious finely chopped and added to soups and stews as well as raw in salads.

As well as being part of the trio of *soffritto* vegetables, celery can be baked in a creamy béchamel sauce or, as they do in Molise, with onions and olives (see page 46). It can be served as part of a crudité selection like the Italian *Pinzimonio,* as well as pickled in *Giardiniera,* the Italian mixed pickles. It can also be blended and made into a lovely pesto (see page 44) and, in Sicily, it is one of the main ingredients of *Caponata*. Like with so many other Italian vegetables, celery can simply be braised and dressed with extra virgin olive oil and lemon juice. Alternatively, I love a simple salad of finely chopped raw celery and celery leaves dressed with extra virgin olive oil, salt, pepper, and dried oregano.

How to use celery:

Buying and storing
Look for firm, tightly packed stalks and, if there are leaves, make sure they look fresh and not wilted. Once home, keep in the salad drawer in the fridge, where it should keep fresh for at least a week.

Preparing
Some of the outer stalks may need to have the stringy bits removed but it's not always necessary.

When using raw celery, try to use the inside sticks near the heart which are the more tender stalks. However, don't discard the outer stalks, use them instead in stocks and soups.

PESTO DI SEDANO
Celery pesto

If you like raw celery, then this is a perfect recipe and a great way of using up leftover celery. You can make the pesto in advance and store it in a sealed container in the fridge for up to 4 days. Try and find celery that still has the leaves attached as they add extra flavor—I know supermarkets tend to trim the leaves off. Use the pesto to dress freshly cooked pasta, or make the Celery Pasta Salad on page 49.

SERVES 4

9½ oz (270 g) celery stalks with leaves
1 garlic clove, peeled
1¾ oz (50 g) walnuts
6 basil leaves
½ cup (50 g) grated Parmesan
⅓ cup (80 ml) extra virgin olive oil
zest of ½ lemon, plus 1 tsp juice
sea salt and freshly ground black pepper

Remove any tough, stringy filaments from the celery stalks, then roughly chop.

Place the chopped celery and celery leaves, the garlic, walnuts, basil, Parmesan, and olive oil in a blender and blend until smooth. Stir in the lemon zest and lemon juice and season to taste.

Add the pesto to freshly cooked pasta or store in the fridge and use when required.

SEDANO ALLA MOLISANA
Baked *celery* with onions and black olives

Celery is an essential part of the *soffritto* in Italian cooking but is often overlooked as a vegetable in its own right. Therefore, I was very curious when I came across this dish from Molise in central Italy. Its roots are firmly in the *cucina povera*; it's very simple to prepare and uses pantry ingredients. I can quite happily eat this as it is with some rustic bread but it also makes a great accompaniment to meat dishes.

SERVES 4

1 whole celery (approx. 8 oz/225 g), cut into 2½ in (6 cm) chunks
2 tbsp extra virgin olive oil, plus extra for greasing
2 large onions, finely sliced
2 tbsp water
50 pitted black olives, whole
2 tbsp dried breadcrumbs
sea salt and freshly ground black pepper

Preheat the oven to 350°F (180°C).

Bring a pot of salted water to a boil and cook the celery for 10 minutes, then drain.

Meanwhile, heat the olive oil in a medium-sized frying pan over medium heat and sweat the onions for about 7 minutes. Add the water, reduce the heat, cover with a lid, and cook for about 20 minutes until softened.

Lightly grease a baking dish (approx. 6¼ in x 8 in/16 cm x 20 cm) with some olive oil. Arrange the celery in the dish, cover with the onions, season with pepper, and scatter over the olives and breadcrumbs.

Cover with foil and cook in the oven for 10 minutes, then remove the foil and continue to cook for 15 minutes.

Remove from the oven and leave to rest for a couple of minutes, then serve.

INSALATA DI PASTA AL SEDANO
Celery pasta salad

In this perfect summer pasta salad, the creamy fresh celery pesto contrasts with the crunchy chopped celery heart. Use the outer celery stalks to make the pesto and the tender heart to add to the pasta salad.

SERVES 4

10½ oz (300 g) farfalle pasta
1 quantity of Celery Pesto (see page 44)
1 celery stalk from the heart, finely sliced, plus leaves for garnishing
12 baby plum or cherry tomatoes, halved
1¾ oz (50 g) provolone dolce cheese, cut into small cubes
sea salt

Bring a large pot of salted water to a boil and cook the pasta until al dente.

Meanwhile, make the celery pesto (see page 44).

Drain the pasta and run under cold water, then transfer to a bowl.

Combine with the pesto, chopped celery heart, tomatoes, and cheese and either serve or store in the fridge until required.

Garnish with chopped celery leaves before serving.

ZUCCHINIS
ZUCCHINE

Zucchinis are much loved in Italy and my fridge is rarely without this very useful vegetable. They belong to the squash family and are, in fact, young marrows that have been picked before they grow too large. Squash originated in Central and South America, but zucchinis were first cultivated in northern Italy in the nineteenth century. They are now grown all over Italy and are a key part of many regional dishes.

Although you can find zucchinis all year round, they are a summer vegetable and are at their best at this time of year when they are tasty, abundant, and cheap. Italy produces quite a few varieties. The most common are bright green, but there is also *Zucchine Chiare,* a lighter green variety with a delicate flavor, and *Zucchine Bianche* from Trieste, which is even paler and suited to being eaten raw.

There are also yellow summer squash but, though pretty to look at, I find them quite bland in flavor. However, you can find beautiful green and white stripy varieties in Italy, which are full of flavor and so pretty to look at when piled high on market stands during the summer. There is also the light green trombone-shaped variety, *Zucchine Trombetta*, which is quite odd looking but delicious combined with potatoes in a stew-type dish. *Zucchine Tonde* is round in shape and ideal for stuffing and roasting, and *Zucchine Romanesche* is popular for its flower.

Zucchinis impart a fresh flavor to any dish and, like eggplants, they are excellent at absorbing the flavors they are cooked with, especially the Mediterranean flavors of the south, like tomatoes, anchovies, chile, and garlic, as well as rich cheesy sauces. I like to use them in a *Parmigiana* in place of eggplants, or they can be filled with meat and leftover stale bread to make them go further (see page 55). Cut into thin strips, dipped in flour, and deep-fried, they make delicious "fries," which kids adore (see page 53), or grated and mixed with some Parmesan, they make lovely fritters.

Zucchinis left whole and boiled, then dressed with extra virgin olive oil and lemon juice, make a comforting light meal for anyone elderly or convalescing from illness. In Naples, they are often cooked *alla scapece*: lightly fried and dressed with extra virgin olive oil, vinegar, garlic, and mint. I like to grate them raw into salads and dress them with balsamic vinegar, or pickle them with other vegetables. You can also use zucchinis in sweet dishes, like *Scarpaccia Viareggina*, a soft pudding-like dessert, or even in cakes (see page 61) and muffins. There really is no end of creative ways to use this wonderful vegetable.

Italians are very fond of zucchini flowers, which they use as much as possible in their cooking during the short season. Simply added to pasta and risotto dishes, or filled with ricotta and herbs and then deep-fried, they are a delicacy and a real treat. Do try and hunt them out as it's such a shame when they are discarded. The best way to obtain them is to grow your own zucchinis, as they can be expensive from specialist grocery stores or farmers' markets.

How to use zucchinis:

Buying and storing
Whatever variety you buy, look for firm, blemish-free zucchinis that are not too big. Large ones are less flavorful and some can be bitter. Obviously, the sooner you use them, the fresher they are, especially if you want to use them raw, but they can be stored in the fridge for a good 4–5 days.

Preparing
They are easy to prepare: simply wash, cut off the hard tops, and either slice or chop according to your recipe. They are quick to cook, either boiled or sautéed, so it really is a fuss-free vegetable.

When stuffing, slice lengthways and, with the help of a small, sharp knife and scoop, remove the inner white flesh. Don't discard the flesh, use it in your filling with the other ingredients.

Zucchini flowers deteriorate very quickly, so are best used on the day of purchase or picking. Otherwise, place them in a glass or vase of water like you would flowers and use them as soon as possible.

ZUCCHINE FRITTE DI ANTONELLA

Antonella's fried *zucchinis*

These light and crunchy fried zucchinis are delicious as a side dish or as a tasty snack with drinks. Be warned though, they are addictive, so you may need to make lots!

SERVES 4–6

1 lb 2 oz (500 g) zucchinis
all-purpose flour, for dusting
abundant vegetable oil, for deep-frying
sea salt

Cut the zucchinis in half across the middle, then cut each half in half again and slice each piece into thin strips. Place all the zucchinis in a bowl, cover with cold water, and leave for 2 hours.

Drain the zucchinis, squeezing out the excess water with your hands. Dust the zucchini strips in all-purpose flour, shaking off any excess.

Heat plenty of vegetable oil in a wide, deep frying pan until hot, then deep-fry the floured zucchini strips, a few at a time, for a couple of minutes until golden. Transfer to paper towels to soak up any excess oil, then sprinkle with salt and serve immediately.

SALTIMBOCCA DI ZUCCHINE
Zucchini saltimbocca

Saltimbocca, meaning "jump in the mouth," usually refers to a thin slice of veal or chicken, which is fried with ham, cheese, and sage. However, this variation substitutes the meat for zucchinis (perfect if you have a seasonal glut) and is baked in the oven. It's a delicious accompaniment to an aperitivo or, served with baby potatoes and a mixed salad, makes a lovely light meal.

MAKES APPROX. 12

1 large zucchini (approx. 12 oz/350 g)
6¼ oz (180 g) fontina cheese
3 oz (80 g) prosciutto slices
a little olive oil, for brushing and drizzling
about 12 sage leaves
sea salt and freshly ground black pepper

Preheat the oven to 400°F (200°C) and line a baking sheet with parchment paper.

Cut the zucchini in half, then cut each half into long, thin (approx. ⅛ in/3 mm) slices. Bring a pot of salted water to a boil, then blanch the zucchini for 2 minutes before transferring to a clean kitchen towel with a slotted spoon. Place another kitchen towel over the top to dry completely.

Cut the fontina into pieces roughly the same size or just a little smaller than the zucchini slices and do the same with the prosciutto.

Brush each zucchini slice with a little olive oil and season with salt and pepper, then place a slice of fontina on top, followed by prosciutto, then top with a sage leaf. Secure the layers with a toothpick as this will prevent the sage leave from flying off in a convection oven.

Place the topped zucchini slices on the prepared baking sheet and bake in the oven for about 7 minutes, until the cheese has melted nicely.

Remove from the oven and serve immediately.

ZUCCHINE RIPIENE
Filled *Zucchinis*

I love to make filled vegetables as it's a great way of making the vegetable go further, and this nutritious dish is so simple to make with just a few everyday ingredients. Depending on the size of your zucchinis, you may not need all the béchamel—decide for yourself once you have mixed everything together. I like to serve this with some roasted baby potatoes and/or a mixed salad.

SERVES 4

4 medium-large zucchinis
1 tbsp extra virgin olive oil, plus extra for greasing and drizzling
1 garlic clove, left whole and squashed
3½ oz (100 g) mushrooms, very finely chopped
1¼ oz (35 g) stale bread, soaked in a little warm water
¼ cup (25 g) grated Parmesan
1 egg yolk
pinch of dried oregano
1 tbsp dried breadcrumbs
sea salt and freshly ground black pepper

For the béchamel sauce
1½ tbsp butter
2 tbsp all-purpose flour
scant 1 cup (200 ml) milk

Preheat the oven to 400°F (200°C). Lightly grease a large baking sheet with a little olive oil.

Cut the zucchinis in half lengthways and carefully scoop out the flesh (to resemble little canoes). Bring a pot of salted water to a boil and quickly blanch the zucchinis for just under a minute, until slightly softened. Lay a clean kitchen towel on a work surface and arrange the zucchini "canoes" upside down to drain and dry out.

Now make the béchamel. Melt the butter in a small saucepan, then remove from the heat and whisk in the flour until you have a smooth paste. Place back on the heat and gradually add the milk, whisking all the time. Continue to whisk over medium-low heat until the sauce thickens, then set aside.

In a small frying pan, heat the olive oil over medium heat and sweat the garlic for a minute, then add the mushrooms and stir-fry for a couple of minutes until cooked. Remove from the heat, discard the garlic, and allow to cool.

Meanwhile, chop the zucchini flesh, squeezing out any excess liquid, then drain the soaked bread and finely chop. Add both to the béchamel sauce, along with the Parmesan, egg yolk, oregano, and cooked mushrooms. Stir to combine and season to taste.

Arrange the zucchini "canoes" on the baking sheet and divide the mixture between them. Sprinkle over the dried breadcrumbs and drizzle with a little olive oil.

Bake in the oven for 35 minutes until golden on top, then serve immediately.

FIORI DI ZUCCA RIPIENI
Filled *Zucchini* Flowers

It is such a shame that zucchini flowers are often discarded; they are such a joy to eat, either filled or chopped and added to soups, pasta, and risotto dishes. Ask for zucchini flowers at the farmers' market, or try growing your own. Serve these with Broccoli Fritters (see page 32) for a fried veggie feast!

SERVES 6

7 oz (200 g) zucchinis
1 egg
6 tbsp grated Parmesan
3 tbsp dried breadcrumbs
handful of basil leaves, finely chopped
6 zucchini flowers, each with baby zucchini attached
sea salt and freshly ground black pepper

For coating and frying
2 eggs
pinch of sea salt
abundant dried breadcrumbs, for coating
abundant vegetable or sunflower oil, for deep-frying

Grate the larger zucchinis and squeeze out the excess liquid with your hands, or a clean kitchen towel if preferred.

Combine the grated zucchini with the egg, Parmesan, breadcrumbs, basil, and some salt and pepper to taste.

Carefully open up the zucchini flowers, ensuring you don't tear the delicate petals.

Remove the interior bud from each one and discard.

Place the filling mixture in a pastry bag and pipe inside each flower. Or, you can do this with a teaspoon if you don't have a pastry bag. Carefully wrap the ends of the flowers around each other so that no filling escapes.

Lightly beat the eggs with a pinch of salt. Dip the stuffed flowers in the egg mixture, then coat in breadcrumbs. Heat plenty of oil in a wide, deep frying pan until hot, then deep-fry the zucchini flowers for 2–3 minutes until golden all over.

Drain on paper towels and serve. These can be eaten hot or cold.

TORTA DOLCE DI ZUCCHINE
Zucchini cake

Healthy and simple to make, this cake is perfect at teatime or even at breakfast with your morning coffee.

SERVES 8–10

10½ oz (300 g) zucchinis
3 eggs
¾ cup (150 g) white sugar
zest of 1 lemon
½ cup (120 ml) sunflower oil
scant ½ cup (60 g) hazelnuts, very finely chopped
2½ cups (300 g) all-purpose flour, sifted
1 x ½ oz (16 g) envelope Paneangeli baking powder, sifted, or use 4 tsp regular baking powder
candied lemon peel (optional)

Preheat the oven to 350°F (180°C). Grease a 9½ in (24 cm) round springform cake pan and line it with parchment paper.

Grate the zucchinis into a colander over a plate or the sink, then cover the grated zucchini with parchment paper or a clean kitchen towel and place a weight (like a can of tomatoes or beans) on top. This will help exude all the liquid from the zucchinis.

In a bowl, beat the eggs and sugar together until light and creamy. Stir in the lemon zest, oil, and hazelnuts, then fold in the flour and *Paneangeli*. Take the zucchinis and, with your hands, squeeze out all the excess liquid, then stir into the cake mixture.

Pour the mixture evenly into the prepared pan, then bake in the oven for 40–45 minutes until risen and golden on top. If you insert a skewer, it should come out clean.

Leave to cool completely before topping with some candied lemon peel. Carefully remove the cake from the pan, then slice and serve.

This cake is best eaten fresh but will keep in an airtight container at room temperature for up to 3 days.

FENNEL
FINOCCHIO

A member of the carrot family, fennel is a native Mediterranean vegetable and is used widely in Italian cuisine, where it is enjoyed both cooked and raw. As we know it today, it consists of a white, fibrous bulb with a green stalk and feathery green leaves. However, it originated as wild fennel and was first grown for its seeds and leaves, which were used as a herb and spice to flavor food. In this way, it was popular with the Ancient Romans, who used the seeds in their cooking as well as for medicinal purposes. Fennel, it was believed, gave you strength. They incorporated it into the gladiators' diet, while the Ancient Greeks fed the seeds to their athletes and often referred to the plant as *marathon*.

Wild fennel grows in abundance in Italy during spring and summer, lining the riverbanks and coastal areas and filling the countryside with its yellow flowers and tall, feathery green leaves. Its distinct aniseed aroma is quite strong and livens up many fish, risotto, and pasta dishes, like the Sicilian *Pasta con le Sarde* (pasta with sardines). And for those who really appreciate fennel's strong flavor, it can be turned into a pesto. Wild fennel leaves are also made into a herbal tea and said to help with digestive problems and soothe an aching belly.

Wild fennel is also found in the countryside and, if I happen upon it on a springtime walk, I will always pick some. However, unless you forage for your own, or are lucky to find it in specialist grocery stores or markets, it is not widely available.

Fennel seeds are used in Italy to flavor sausages and cured meats, like the Tuscan *finocchiona* salami, and are a typical ingredient added to *taralli*—small, bread-like snacks. They are also widely used in South Asian cooking and are readily available in the spice sections of most grocery stores.

The domesticated fennel that we know today has been growing in Italy for at least the last couple of centuries. This bulb fennel, known as Florentine, is mainly grown in southern Italy. It flourishes during late fall and winter and is much sweeter in taste than the wild variety. It is the bulb that is used to cook with and, although not as aromatic as the wild variety, the stalk can be added to stocks and soups in the same way as celery, and the fronds used for a garnish.

The thick bulb is delicious eaten raw; finely sliced and added to salads. A particular favorite is the refreshing Sicilian salad of fennel and oranges, sometimes with the addition of anchovies and black olives. Or you could simply dress sliced fennel with extra virgin olive oil and season with salt and pepper for a nice refreshing side salad or healthy snack. Fennel is sometimes eaten like a piece of fruit at the end of a rich meal as it is believed to help with digestion.

Fennel is equally delicious cooked: braised in milk (see page 65), baked with Parmesan and breadcrumbs, blended in a soup (see page 64), or added to pasta, risotto, or stews. It can be roasted and served as a side dish with a Sunday dinner, or dipped in batter and deep-fried, or coated in breadcrumbs and baked or grilled like a steak (see page 67).

How to use fennel:

Buying and storing
Try to buy fennel during the fall or winter when it is abundant and at its best. Look for hard, well-rounded bulbs without blemishes. Once home, use on the same day or store in the salad drawer of the fridge for about 3 days.

Preparing
Using a sharp knife, slice off the stalks and fronds and reserve these to use in stocks and soups. Remove the root end and the tougher outer layer of the bulb, then slice the bulb in half lengthways and cut out the hard core. Use immediately or place in acidulated water to prevent discoloration. If you are baking or roasting fennel, it is best to blanch it in water first for a few minutes, otherwise the flesh will remain hard.

VELLUTATA DI FINOCCHI
Fennel Soup

This delicious soup is so simple to prepare and can be made in advance and frozen. The addition of potato and Parmesan makes it lovely and creamy as well as nutritious.

SERVES 4

2 lb (900 g) fennel
¼ cup (60 ml) extra virgin olive oil
1 onion, finely chopped
2 oz (60 g) pancetta, roughly chopped (optional)
5¼ oz (150 g) potato, peeled and roughly chopped into small chunks
3 cups (700 ml) hot vegetable stock
6 tbsp grated Parmesan
freshly ground black pepper

Remove the outer leaves, stem, and green fronds from the fennel bulbs, reserving the fronds. Roughly chop the fennel bulbs and set aside.

Heat the olive oil in a heavy-based pot over medium heat and sweat the onion and pancetta (if using) for about 5 minutes. Stir in the potato and cook for a minute, then add the fennel and a little black pepper and stir-fry over medium-low heat for 10 minutes.

Add the hot vegetable stock and bring to a boil, then lower the heat, stir in the Parmesan, and simmer, covered with a lid, for 30 minutes, until the fennel is tender and cooked through.

Remove from the heat and blend until smooth. Gently reheat if necessary and serve garnished with the green fennel fronds.

FINOCCHI AL LATTE
Fennel cooked in milk

In this popular Italian side dish, the fennel is cooked in milk, which tenderizes it and brings out its delicate flavor but also adds a lovely creaminess. Traditionally, it's served alongside roast meats or fish dishes, but you could enjoy it as a main dish with perhaps a mixed salad and some rustic bread.

SERVES 2–4 (2 AS A MAIN OR 4 AS A SIDE)

1 lb 2 oz (500 g) fennel (either 1 large or 2 small)
1½ tbsp butter
1 tbsp extra virgin olive oil
½ cup (240 ml) milk
¼ cup (30 g) grated Parmesan
sea salt and freshly ground black pepper
zest of ½ lemon, to serve

Remove the hard outer layer of the fennel, the stem, and green fronds, then slice the bulb in half if you are using a large fennel, or keep the small ones intact. Bring a pot of salted water to a boil and cook the fennel for 3 minutes, then remove from the heat, drain well, and dry on a clean kitchen towel. When dry, slice into segments about ½ in (1 cm) thick.

In a frying pan, heat the butter and olive oil and fry the fennel segments over high heat for 2–3 minutes on each side until golden. Season with a little salt and pepper.

In a bowl or jug, combine the milk and Parmesan with a little black pepper, then pour over the fennel and cook over high heat for about 10 minutes, until the milk has been absorbed.

Remove from the heat and serve with a sprinkling of lemon zest.

FINOCCHI IMPANATI CON INSALATA D'ARANCE
Fennel "steaks" served with an orange salad

These crispy fennel slices make great "steaks" and, as fennel and orange go really well together, I like to serve them with a refreshing orange salad. I have baked them for a healthier option, but you could deep-fry them, if you prefer.

SERVES 4

2 large or 4 small fennel
3 eggs
3½ oz (100 g) dried breadcrumbs
¼ cup (30 g) grated Parmesan
needles of 1 rosemary sprig, finely chopped
all-purpose flour, for dusting
a little extra virgin olive oil, for drizzling
sea salt and freshly ground black pepper

For the orange salad
2 large oranges (regular or blood), peeled and pith removed
2 tsp capers
11 pitted black olives
4 anchovy fillets (optional)
1½ tbsp extra virgin olive oil
sea salt and freshly ground black pepper

Preheat the oven to 400°F (200°C). Line a baking sheet with parchment paper.

Remove the hard outer layer of the fennel and cut in half lengthways, then cut each half into slices about ½ in (1 cm) thick. Place on a plate and sprinkle with a little salt.

In a bowl, lightly beat the eggs with a little salt. In another dish, combine the breadcrumbs, Parmesan, rosemary, and some black pepper.

Pat dry the fennel slices with paper towels or a clean kitchen towel, then dust in some flour, dip in the egg, and coat in the breadcrumb mixture (pressing down with your hands on both sides to ensure the fennel is well coated).

Transfer the fennel to the lined baking sheet, drizzle with a little olive oil, and bake in the oven for 20–25 minutes, turning them over halfway through, until both sides are golden.

Meanwhile, make the orange salad. Cut the oranges into slices and arrange on a plate with the capers, black olives, and anchovy fillets (if using). Sprinkle with salt and pepper and drizzle with the olive oil.

Serve the crispy fennel steaks straight from the oven, along with the salad.

GREEN BEANS
FAGIOLINI

The story goes that green beans (or a closely related type) originated in Central and South America and were brought to Europe by Christopher Columbus. In Italian, the word *fagiolini* means "little beans" and refers to what is inside the pod. However, the pod is so tender that the whole thing is consumed. This tenderness has evolved over time and, therefore, these days the majority of young green beans do not have a tough string that needs to be removed.

Also known as *cornetti* and *tegolina*, depending on which region you are in, there are many types of green beans in Italy and in different colors, too—white, yellow, purple—some fat, some flat. The most popular green variety, which we all know and love, grows all over Italy but predominantly in Emilia Romagna, Sicily, Veneto, and Piemonte. Veneto is also known for its "meaty" whitish/yellow variety *Meraviglia di Venezia*.

Although flown in from all parts of the world, green beans are a late spring and summer vegetable and are a must during the summer when they are abundant and at their best. They are easy to grow and often a favorite in backyard and community gardens—there is nothing more delicious than freshly picked steamed green beans; you really need nothing else to enhance the flavor.

Italians enjoy green beans in many dishes. Lightly cooked, they make a wonderful salad when combined with baby potatoes and dressed with extra virgin olive oil and mint. They are also delicious stewed with tomatoes (see page 70), or baked with cheese (see page 72), or stir-fried with oil and garlic and topped with breadcrumbs. They take center stage in the Ligurian dish of *Trofie* with potatoes and pesto, or in a *Condiglione* salad, which is the Ligurian version of the French *Niçoise* salad, with tuna, potato, red onion, peppers, and black olives.

How to use green beans:

Buying and storing
Look for beans that are bright in color and firm, without any blemishes. Try one; if it snaps easily, it will be fresh and tasty. Once home, store in the salad drawer of your fridge for about 4 days.

Preparing
Using a sharp knife, simply trim off the ends. However, if your beans are really fresh and tender, then you can leave the curly ends on as they look very pretty, especially in a salad. Cook whole or chopped up into shorter lengths in plenty of salted boiling water for about 5 minutes (if you like to have them quite crunchy). Italians like green beans well cooked, so will often boil them for longer (15–20 minutes, depending on size).

FAGIOLINI ALLA PIZZAIOLA
Green beans with tomatoes

This makes the perfect end-of-summer dish, when green beans and tomatoes are in abundance. Serve as an accompaniment to meat or fish or simply eat as a main course with lots of good bread to mop up the sauce.

SERVES 2–4

7 oz (200 g) trimmed green beans
2 tbsp extra virgin olive oil
1 garlic clove, finely sliced
½ red chile, finely chopped
2 basil stalks, finely chopped
9 oz (250 g) baby plum tomatoes, cut in half
½ tsp dried oregano
½ handful of basil leaves, whole
sea salt

Bring a pot of salted water to a boil and cook the green beans for about 7 minutes until tender.

Meanwhile, heat the olive oil in a pan over medium heat and sweat the garlic, chile, and basil stalks. Stir in the tomatoes and oregano with a little salt, then cover with a lid and cook for a couple of minutes until slightly softened.

Drain the beans and add them to the tomatoes with about 4 tablespoons of the cooking water, then cover with a lid again and cook over medium-low heat for 3 minutes.

Serve immediately with freshly torn basil leaves.

SFORMATO DI FAGIOLINI
Green bean bake

This savory bake enriches green beans with delicious melted cheese. I have used a mild provolone known as *dolce* and Parmesan, but you could use whatever cheese you have lying around and you could also add chopped pieces of cured meat, if you like. I like to serve it with a crunchy mixed salad.

SERVES 4

1½ tbsp butter, plus extra for greasing and dotting
4 tsp dried breadcrumbs, plus extra for dusting
1 lb 2 oz (500 g) potatoes, peeled and cut into small chunks
8½ oz (240 g) trimmed green beans
1¾ oz (50 g) provolone dolce cheese, cut into small cubes
2 eggs
leaves of 2 small thyme sprigs
6 tbsp grated Parmesan
sea salt and freshly ground black pepper

Preheat the oven to 350°F (180°C). Lightly grease a baking dish (approx. 8 in x 8 in/20 cm x 20 cm) with a little butter and dust with breadcrumbs.

Bring a pot of salted water to a boil and cook the potatoes and green beans for about 10 minutes until tender, then drain well and steam-dry the potatoes. When dry, mash the potatoes with the butter and roughly chop the green beans.

In a bowl, combine the mashed potatoes and beans with the provolone, eggs, thyme leaves, and three-quarters of the Parmesan, then season to taste.

Spread the mixture evenly into the prepared baking dish. Combine the breadcrumbs with the remaining grated Parmesan and sprinkle this all over the top, then dot with butter.

Bake in the oven for 35 minutes until golden, then serve straight away.

LEEKS
PORRI

Belonging to the *Liliaceae* family, which includes the flowering lily, leeks are part of the Allium species, which includes onion, garlic, and chives. They have a milder, sweeter taste than an onion and so are often used as a substitute.

The leek has been around since ancient times and the Romans certainly made good use of this vegetable. In fact, it is said that the emperor Nero believed leeks would improve his voice and so ate them daily, which earned him the nickname *Porophagus* (leek eater). I cannot attest to its voice-improving properties but it is certainly high in fiber and many essential nutrients.

Leeks have always grown well in Mediterranean areas and, as they spread throughout Europe, it became apparent that they also thrived in cooler climates. Indeed, they became a national symbol of Wales.

Like white asparagus, leeks are "blanched" while they grow. This process excludes light to prevent photosynthesis and the production of chlorophyll and therefore a large proportion of the stem stays white. It is the white and light green parts that are used in cooking, although the darker green tops can be added to flavor stocks. Grown all over Italy, but especially in central and northern regions, the best time for leeks is November through to March.

Like onions, leeks are often sautéed with other vegetables in a *soffritto*, as a base for soups, stews, and sauces. However, unlike the onion, the leek's sweet flavor makes it an ideal vegetable to serve on its own, simply cooked in a little butter or olive oil. I also like to dress them with *agrodolce* (a sticky sweet and sour Italian sauce, see page 77).

Leeks pair well with pancetta and these are often combined in soups, like minestrone, or pasta or risotto dishes. Leeks also make a lovely gratin with creamy béchamel sauces, and are used in savory pies and quiche-type tarts with ricotta or strong cheeses like Gorgonzola, Taleggio, or Parmesan.

How to use leeks:

Buying and storing
Where possible, look for small tender ones; larger leeks aren't necessarily the best or freshest. Make sure they are firm without blemishes and not yellowing. I find they are best eaten on the day of purchase, but can be stored in the fridge for 3–4 days.

Preparing
Using a sharp knife, cut off the green tops and trim the hard base, then remove the outer layer and rinse well under cold running water. Slice according to your recipe and then rinse again in fresh cold water; earth has a tendency to get trapped within the leaves. If you're cooking leeks whole, don't trim the hard base as the leaves will fall apart.

Leeks are very quick to cook and, when sliced, will boil in a couple of minutes. Frying should only take 3–4 minutes. However, cook gently and don't allow them to brown, otherwise they will taste bitter. Whole leeks take a little longer; about 20 minutes if boiling and 40 minutes if roasting.

ZUPPA DI PORRI E CANNELLINI
Leek and cannellini bean soup

This delicate creamy soup can be made with just pantry ingredients. Pancetta adds flavor but you can omit it, if you prefer. The addition of Parmesan rind is a great way to make use of all of the cheese.

SERVES 4

1 lb 5 oz (600 g) leeks
3 tbsp extra virgin olive oil, plus extra to drizzle
1 onion, finely sliced
1 oz (30 g) pancetta, finely chopped (optional)
1 tsp red pepper flakes
2 whole rosemary sprigs
2 medium-sized potatoes, peeled and cut into small chunks
2 x 14 oz (400 g) cans cannellini beans
2½ oz (70 g) Parmesan rind, cut into small cubes
5 cups (1.2 liters) hot vegetable stock

Prepare the leeks by removing the first layer and discarding the tough base, then slicing into thin rounds.

Heat the olive oil in a heavy-based pot and sweat the onion, pancetta (if using), and red pepper flakes with the needles of 1 rosemary sprig. Cook for a couple of minutes, then stir in the leeks, reserving about a handful for later.

Add the potatoes and cook over medium heat for 5 minutes until softened. Stir in the beans with the liquid from the cans, along with the Parmesan rind and hot stock. Bring to a boil, then reduce the heat and simmer gently for 15 minutes, partially covered with a lid. Remove from the heat and blend until smooth.

Heat a drizzle of olive oil in a small frying pan and stir-fry the reserved leeks with the remaining rosemary sprig until softened and golden.

Gently reheat the soup if necessary, then divide among individual bowls and garnish with a little of the stir-fried leek.

PORRI ALL'AGRODOLCE
Leeks agrodolce (sweet and sour)

Cooking *agrodolce* means using wine vinegar and sugar and is the Italian equivalent of sweet and sour. Leeks are perfect for this method and this dish makes a lovely antipasto or can be served with drinks together with a plate of cheese and cured meats. As with any *agrodolce* dish, making it a day or two in advance will enhance the flavor.

SERVES 4–6

4 leeks
¼ cup (60 ml) extra virgin olive oil
2 tbsp water (optional)
sea salt
2 tbsp white wine vinegar
4 tsp sugar, whatever type you have on hand
2 tsp capers
10 pitted green olives, cut in half

Prepare the leeks by removing the first layer and discarding the tough base, then slicing into thin rounds.

Heat the olive oil in a frying pan and sweat the leeks over medium-low heat for about 5 minutes until softened, taking care not to let them burn. Add the water, if necessary.

Add a little salt to taste, then increase the heat and add the vinegar, sugar, capers, and olives. When you've cooked off the vinegar and the sugar has dissolved, reduce the heat, cover with a lid, and continue to cook for 5 minutes.

Leave to marinate for at least 30 minutes, then reheat and serve hot or enjoy cold.

PEAS
PISELLI

The sweet flavor of fresh peas is always a joy and a sure sign that spring and better weather have finally arrived. Market stalls, piled high with bright green pods, is then a familiar sight in Italy and Italians certainly make the most of them for their short season.

The wild pea has been in existence for thousands of years, probably originating in Asia. Wild peas were grown for their seeds, which were mashed and cooked with grains, as well as ground to make flour for bread. As the pea evolved and cultivation began, field peas were grown in much the same way as the wild pea, and then dried to provide fodder for livestock, as well as for human consumption.

The more sophisticated white-flowering garden pea was adopted by the Greeks, as well as the Ancient Romans, and became a food for the rich, leaving the field pea for the masses. In the Middle Ages, during the time of the Italian city-states, peas became a symbol of good fortune and prosperity for the city of Venice and, on the feast of St. Mark's each year, a plate of *Risi e Bisi* (rice and peas) was eaten in celebration. This broth-type risotto dish is still popular in the Venice region today.

Peas are grown almost everywhere in Italy and, because of their high protein and fiber content, they are often considered a legume (pulse). In fact, the dish *Pasta e Piselli* (pasta with peas) is a typical example of *cucina povera,* where peas provided protein in place of meat. It still is a very popular dish in the Italian kitchen, often with the addition of pancetta and mint or basil, and lots of Parmesan or pecorino cheese.

Peas are indispensable in the kitchen today and we are lucky to be able to enjoy them frozen, dried, and even canned all year round. Many pasta and risotto dishes include peas (see page 80), as well as soups like minestrone, or they can be blended to make a *vellutata* (creamy soup). They can also be mashed and made into *polpette* (see page 82), or added to cheesy bakes, meat or vegetable stews, lamb dishes, or simply to bulk out tomato sauces. Peas combine well with pancetta or prosciutto and, together with onions, are often simply sautéed and presented as a side dish. Very fresh tender peas are delicious eaten raw and are often added to salads.

In Italy, dried peas are popular during the winter when the fresh variety is not available. Often cooked and then mashed into soups, they have a stronger taste and you would be forgiven for mistaking them for a completely different ingredient! In fact, they are very similar to the original field pea and come in green or yellow, whole or split. Split dried peas have their skins removed to speed up the cooking process. However, both types take longer to cook than the frozen or fresh variety and may need overnight soaking. Their protein content is much higher and these nutritious pulses are often used in the same way as lentils or chickpeas.

Tacole is also a popular type of pea. In the UK, we know it by its French name, *mangetout*, and in North America it is known as the snow pea. This type has been specially developed and is picked very young, while still flat, so the whole pod can be eaten. Simply remove the string and cook whole in stir-fries or blanch for a couple of minutes and add to salads. Sugar snaps are also a variety of young, crunchy pea. The entire pod is edible and it is used in a similar way.

How to use peas:

Buying and storing

Look for firm, bright shiny green pods and beware of any blemishes or yellowing as this means they are old and not fresh. Once home, it is best to use them on the day as they tend to lose their fresh taste and their sugars turn into starch. Otherwise, store them in the fridge as keeping them cool slows this process down a little, but use as soon as possible. There is a lot of wastage with fresh peas as the pods are generally not used, so make sure you buy enough; if your recipe asks for 9 oz (250 g) of shelled peas, make sure you buy at least double the weight of pods.

Preparing

Cooking fresh peas takes a little longer than the frozen variety, so bear this in mind when following a recipe. Industrially frozen peas are blanched and then frozen immediately in order to retain as much freshness and nutrient-value as possible. They really are so handy to keep in the freezer. You don't need to pod them, they're inexpensive, and you can use them all year round. I have therefore used frozen peas in all the recipes in this book. Generally, there are two different types—larger garden peas and the smaller ones known as petits pois. Both are good and it's really up to you which you prefer.

RISOTTO CREMOSO DI PISELLI E MENTA
Creamy *pea* and mint risotto

I always keep risotto rice in my pantry and peas in the freezer, so this makes a quick and easy meal for me at any time. Blending half of the peas makes the risotto even creamier and contrasts nicely with the texture of the whole peas. The addition of mint also adds a pleasant freshness.

SERVES 4

5 tbsp extra virgin olive oil
1 small onion, very finely chopped
3 cups (400 g) frozen peas
sea salt
½ handful of mint leaves, roughly chopped
1½ cups (300 g) arborio rice
⅓ cup (80 ml) white wine
5 cups (1.2 liters) hot vegetable stock
2 tbsp butter
6 tbsp grated Parmesan

Heat 3 tablespoons of olive oil in a frying pan over medium heat and sweat three-quarters of the onion for a couple of minutes until softened. Add the peas with a little salt and three-quarters of the mint leaves, then reduce the heat and cook for about 4 minutes until the peas are cooked.

Remove the pan from the heat, transfer half of the pea mixture to a blender, and blend until smooth.

In a heavy-based pot, heat the remaining olive oil over medium heat and sweat the remaining onion for a couple of minutes until softened. Stir in the rice, coating each grain with oil. Add the wine, stir, and allow to evaporate. Add a ladle of hot stock and the mashed peas, reduce the heat, and stir until the liquid has been absorbed. Add another ladle of hot stock and, stirring continuously, cook like this for about 17–20 minutes, gradually adding more stock, until the rice is cooked al dente. Towards the end of the cooking time, stir in the whole peas and remaining chopped mint.

When the risotto is cooked, remove from the heat, mix in the butter and grated Parmesan, and serve immediately.

Green Vegetables

POLPETTE DI PISELLI CON SALSA PICCANTE AL POMODORO

Pea polpette served with a spicy tomato sauce

These little pea polpette are light, delicate, and full of nutritious ingredients.

MAKES 15

2⅓ cups (320 g) frozen peas
½ cup (100 g) ricotta
¾ cup (90 g) dried breadcrumbs
¼ cup (30 g) grated Parmesan
1 egg, beaten
1 small garlic clove, finely diced
5 mint leaves, finely chopped
sea salt and freshly ground black pepper

For the tomato sauce
1 tbsp extra virgin olive oil
1 garlic clove, crushed
½ red chile, finely chopped
1 x 14 oz (400 g) can chopped tomatoes
pinch of sea salt

Bring a pot of salted water to a boil and cook the peas for about 7 minutes until well cooked, then drain well and blend until smooth. Transfer to a bowl and leave to cool.

Stir the ricotta into the peas, along with ¼ cup (30 g) of the breadcrumbs, the Parmesan, egg, garlic, and mint. Season, then place in the fridge for 30–40 minutes, until the mixture sets slightly.

Preheat the oven to 400°F (200°C) and line a baking sheet with parchment paper.

Now make the tomato sauce. Heat the olive oil in a heavy-based pan over medium heat and sweat the garlic and chile for a minute, then add the tomatoes with a pinch of salt and cook gently for about 25 minutes, partially covered with a lid.

Meanwhile, form small handfuls of the ricotta mixture into golf ball-sized balls. Place the remaining breadcrumbs on a plate and roll each ball to coat, then place on the lined baking sheet and bake in the oven for 15 minutes, until they color slightly and start to crack.

Serve with the spicy tomato sauce.

TORTINO DI PISELLI
Pea soufflés

These pea soufflés won't collapse when you take them out of the oven (like most soufflés do) so they are perfect for a dinner party, or a simple midweek family meal.

MAKES 6

2 tbsp butter, plus extra for greasing
1 tbsp extra virgin olive oil
2 small shallots, finely chopped
4½ cups (600 g) frozen peas
2 eggs, separated
⅔ cup (150 g) ricotta
½ cup (50 g) grated Parmesan
sea salt and freshly ground black pepper
pea shoots to finish (optional)

Preheat the oven to 350°F (180°C).

Heat the butter and olive oil in a frying pan over medium heat and sweat the shallots for about 3 minutes until softened, then stir in the peas and cook for 5–7 minutes until tender. Remove from the heat and allow to cool slightly.

Meanwhile, whisk the egg whites until stiff, then set aside.

Scoop 4 tablespoons of the cooked pea mixture into a bowl and set aside, then blend the rest to a smooth purée.

Place the ricotta, Parmesan, and egg yolks in a large bowl. Mix in the blended peas and season with salt and pepper, then fold in the stiffened egg whites and whole peas.

Grease 6 ramekin dishes with butter and divide the mixture among them. Place the ramekins in a baking dish or roasting pan and fill with hot water to reach halfway up the ramekins. Bake in the oven for 30 minutes until well risen and slightly golden, with cracks forming on the top.

Remove from the oven, lift the ramekins out of the dish/pan, and carefully flip over onto a serving dish, or you can serve directly in the ramekins. Top with pea shoots, if you like.

ARUGULA
RUCOLA

Known in Italian as *rucola, rughetta,* or *ruchetta* (derived from the Latin *eruca*), this peppery-tasting green leaf makes a lovely addition to salads but is delicious in cooked dishes, too.

Native to the Mediterranean and Asia, arugula was known to the Ancient Egyptians and Romans, who used its pungent aroma to flavor dishes and believed it to be an aphrodisiac. Belonging to the brassica family, like cabbage and broccoli, it is rich in vitamins and so has many health benefits.

Arugula has been growing wild for centuries and its pretty yellow flowers are a common sight on country walks in the spring. The wild variety has thinner, longer leaves than the cultivated variety, and tends to be stronger in flavor. It is very easy to grow and, since its revival in the 1980s, has become a somewhat "trendy" leaf, so it is now cultivated all over the world.

Apart from adding a few leaves to salads, the classic restaurant-style way of serving a arugula salad is to dress it with olive oil and balsamic vinegar and shave a little Parmesan over the top. However, in Italy, arugula is often added to pasta and risotto (see page 89) and used to fill ravioli as well as savory pies and tarts (see page 90). When cooked, arugula loses its pungent peppery taste. If you wish to retain the flavor and the freshness, simply add the arugula at the last minute so it doesn't actually cook. An arugula pesto is used to dress pasta, or as a topping for bruschetta, or an accompaniment to fish. Arugula leaves make a wonderful topping for beef carpaccio and freshly-baked pizza (see page 87), and also go well with prosciutto, mozzarella, and tomatoes in *panini*.

How to use arugula:

Buying and storing
Unless you grow or pick your own, arugula leaves are easily obtainable, ready-prepped in bags, in the salad section of supermarkets. Make sure the leaves are bright green with no signs of yellowing. Store in the salad drawer of your fridge for no more than 2 or 3 days.

PIZZA BIANCA CON SCAMORZA E RUCOLA
Pizza with scamorza and *arugula*

Known as *pizza bianca* ("white pizza") in Italy because it doesn't use tomato sauce, this simple pizza is made with *scarmorza*, a smoky cheese that resembles hard mozzarella. The addition of anchovies and capers gives it a nice kick and the arugula adds a lovely freshness. If you prefer, you can divide the pizza dough into four and make the pizzas smaller.

MAKES 2 LARGE ROUND PIZZAS, APPROX. 12¾ IN (32 CM) IN DIAMETER

9 oz (250 g) scamorza cheese, cut into small cubes
2 tsp capers
4 anchovy fillets, roughly chopped
¼ cup (60 ml) extra virgin olive oil
juice of ½ lemon
3 cups (60 g) arugula
sea salt and freshly ground black pepper

For the dough
4 cups (500 g) strong bread flour, plus extra for dusting
2 tsp sea salt
1 x ¼ oz (7 g) envelope of fast-acting instant yeast
approx. 1⅓ cups (325 ml) lukewarm water

First make the dough. In a large bowl, mix the flour, salt, and dried yeast, then gradually stir in the lukewarm water to make a dough. Knead for 10 minutes, then cover with a cloth and leave to rest for 10 minutes.

Divide the dough in half and knead each piece for a couple of minutes, cover each with a cloth, and leave to rise in a warm place for about 1 hour, or until doubled in size.

Preheat the oven to 460°F (240°C).

In a bowl, combine the scamorza, capers, anchovies, and 2 tablespoons of olive oil and season with pepper and a little salt.

On a lightly floured work surface, roll out each piece of dough into an even circle approximately 12¾ in (32 cm) in diameter. Place the pizza bases on baking sheets (or use a pizza stone), top with the scamorza mixture, and bake in the hot oven for about 10 minutes until the crust is cooked through.

Meanwhile, mix together the remaining olive oil with the lemon juice and season with salt and pepper, then toss through the arugula.

Top the cooked pizzas with the arugula and serve.

RISOTTO CON RUCOLA E TALEGGIO

Risotto with *arugula* and Taleggio cheese

The lovely peppery fresh arugula enhances the creaminess of this simple risotto Enriched with the northern Italian cheese, Taleggio, it is a meal in itself.

SERVES 4

3 tbsp extra virgin olive oil
1 small onion, finely chopped
1¾ cups (350 g) arborio rice
⅓ cup (80 ml) white wine
approx. 6⅓ cups (1.5 liters) hot vegetable stock
4¼ oz (120 g) Taleggio cheese, roughly chopped
2½ oz (70 g) arugula, plus a few extra leaves to garnish
2 tbsp butter

Heat the olive oil in a heavy-based saucepan over medium heat and sweat the onion for a couple of minutes until softened. Stir in the rice until each grain is coated in the oil, then add the white wine and allow to evaporate.

Gradually add the hot stock, one ladle at a time, stirring continuously with a wooden spoon until the rice has absorbed the liquid. Continue cooking in this way for 15–17 minutes, until the rice is al dente.

Remove from the heat, stir in the taleggio cheese until it has melted, then stir in the arugula, followed by the butter. Garnish with a few extra arugula leaves before serving immediately.

TORTA SALATA DI RUCOLA
Arugula tart

The pastry for this tart is often known as *pasta matta* in Italy and is simply made with flour, butter, and water. Arugula is added to the tart mixture as well as placed on the bottom of the pastry and added fresh once the tart is cooked. It is simple, fresh, and perfect for a light meal during spring and summer when arugula is in abundance. However, as arugula is usually available to buy in supermarkets all year round, it can also be enjoyed anytime. The pecorino marries perfectly with the peppery arugula and tangy sun-dried tomatoes. If you can't find pecorino, simply use Parmesan or any other hard cheese you have on hand.

SERVES 4–6

For the pastry
1⅔ cups (200 g) all-purpose flour, sifted, plus extra for dusting
7 tbsp (100 g) cold butter, cut into small pieces, plus extra for greasing
approx. 5 tbsp cold water

For the filling
3½ cups (70 g) arugula
generous 1 cup (250 g) ricotta
1 tsp lemon zest, plus extra for sprinkling
½ cup (30 g) sun-dried tomatoes, finely chopped, plus a couple extra to garnish
3 tbsp grated pecorino cheese
2 eggs
sea salt and freshly ground black pepper

First make the pastry. Sift the flour into a bowl, add the pieces of butter, and rub in with your fingertips until it resembles breadcrumbs. Gradually add enough cold water and mix with your hands to obtain a smooth dough. Roll the dough into a ball and leave to rest in the fridge while you make the filling.

Preheat the oven to 400°F (200°C) and lightly grease a 9½ in (24 cm) round loose-bottomed tart pan with butter, then dust it with flour.

Finely chop almost half of the arugula and combine in a bowl with the ricotta, lemon zest, sun-dried tomatoes, pecorino, eggs, and a little salt and pepper.

On a lightly floured work surface, roll out the pastry and line the bottom and sides of the prepared tart pan. With a fork, make lots of indentations all over the pastry. Scatter over half of the remaining arugula to cover the base, then pour in the creamy mixture. Bake in the oven for 25–30 minutes, until the filling has risen and turned golden.

Remove from the oven, leave to rest for 5 minutes, then carefully remove from the pan. Top with the remaining arugula, chopped sun-dried tomatoes, and lemon zest, then slice and serve.

SALAD GREENS
INSALATE

Often, when one thinks of salad, a sad pile of limp green leaves on the side of a plate can come to mind. This is such a shame as the salad leaf is a wonderful ingredient and there is such an array to choose from—different shapes, sizes, flavors, and textures in various shades of green, some tinged ruby red. Romaine lettuce, gem, iceberg, butterhead, frisée, curly endive, lamb's lettuce, watercress, and so many other varieties are available throughout the year. These leaves are full of flavor and nutrients and can form the basis of many salads or be used to make wonderful creamy soups, or flavor pasta and risotto dishes and savory pies.

These days, salad heads are generally available to buy all year round but it is in early spring, when fresh young leaves begin to emerge, that they are at their best. In Italy, it is common for people to forage for wild salad green varieties like dandelion, wild garlic, arugula, and sorrel.

Italians love *puntarelle*, a bitter-tasting salad-type vegetable from the chicory family, also known as *Cicoria Catalogna*. This is very popular in Rome during the winter and early spring. It looks almost like celery at first glance, with long pale stalks and green pointy leaves. However, hidden inside the outer leaves is the heart—a gnarled cluster of tightly packed, green, unopened buds. The best way to enjoy their crisp freshness is in a salad (see page 95) but it is also delicious with pasta (see page 96) so, if you are able to find them, you're in for a treat. The preparation takes a bit of time but it is so well worth it (see right).

How to use salad greens:

Buying and storing
When buying salad greens, look for fresh, crisp heads without blemishes or signs of discoloration. Store in the salad drawer of your fridge and use within a couple of days. If you notice the leaves turning limp, blend them into a soup or sauté them with olive oil, garlic, and chile.

Preparing puntarelle
Remove the outer leaves to reveal the heart and slice the buds into thin strips. In Italy, a specially made wire cutter is used for this, but a good, small sharp knife will do the job. Soak the leaves in ice-cold water for at least 30 minutes, until they begin to curl. This helps to remove some of the bitterness and will also look pretty when plated. Dress with olive oil, salt and pepper, diced garlic, and anchovies, which is the perfect dressing to complement the slight bitterness. Don't discard the outer leaves, add them to soups, stews, and pasta dishes.

Dressing
There are many salad dressing variations worldwide, but Italians prefer a simple dressing of good olive oil with wine vinegar or lemon juice and a sprinkling of salt. The usual ratio is half the quantity of vinegar or lemon juice to olive oil. And remember—a fresh salad, once dressed, should be consumed right away.

VELLUTATA DI LATTUGA E CRESCIONE
Lettuce and watercress *soup*

This nourishing soup is a great way of using up any leftover lettuce. Here, I use the economical iceberg lettuce, a gem lettuce, and a couple of bags of watercress, but you can use whatever you have on hand. The addition of potatoes helps to thicken the soup without the need for any cream. Serve with homemade croutons or simply with some rustic bread for a lovely lunch of "green" goodness.

SERVES 4

2 tbsp extra virgin olive oil
1 leek, finely sliced
2 iceberg lettuce heads, broken up
1 gem lettuce, broken up
  (total combined lettuce approx.
  1 lb 2 oz/500 g)
5¾ oz (160 g) watercress
2 medium-sized potatoes (approx.
  8½ oz/240 g), cut into small chunks
4¼ cups (1 liter) hot vegetable stock
pat of butter
leaves of 2 small thyme sprigs
4 slices of rustic bread, cut into small
  chunks (for croûtons)
sea salt and freshly ground black pepper

Heat the olive oil in a heavy-based pot over medium heat and sweat the leek for a minute or so until softened. Add all the lettuce leaves, watercress, and potatoes and mix well together. Pour in the hot stock, bring to a boil, then reduce the heat, cover with a lid, and cook gently for 20 minutes.

Remove from the heat and blend until smooth. Check the seasoning and add salt and pepper, if desired.

Melt the butter in a frying pan with the thyme leaves, add the bread chunks, and fry on all sides until golden.

If necessary, gently reheat the soup, then serve with the croûtons.

INSALATA DI PUNTARELLE E PANE
Puntarelle and bread *salad*

The crunchiness of the puntarelle shoots combines really well with the softened bread to make a type of *Panzanella* salad. The addition of sun-dried tomatoes brings a nice strong flavor and the eggs add protein, making this a light but complete meal.

SERVES 4

1 bunch of puntarelle (approx. 1 lb 10 oz/750 g total weight)
scant 1 cup (200 ml) water
¼ cup (60 ml) red or white wine vinegar
10½ oz (300 g) stale rustic bread, lightly toasted and cut into small chunks
5 tbsp extra virgin olive oil, plus extra for drizzling
2 garlic cloves, finely chopped
½ red chile, finely sliced
10 sun-dried tomatoes, finely sliced
2 cold hard-boiled eggs, peeled and quartered
sea salt

Remove the outer green leaves of the puntarelle until you get to the harder white shoots inside. Cut off the base and thinly slice lengthways, then plunge into ice-cold water—this will make them curl. Reserve the outer green leaves to use in another recipe (see Trofie Pasta with Puntarelle on page 96), or you could add them to soups.

Combine the water and vinegar and then pour over the bread. Leave to rest for a couple of minutes, then squeeze out any excess liquid.

In a small jug, combine the olive oil with the garlic, chile, and a little salt.

Drain the puntarelle and pat dry with a clean kitchen towel. Place in a large bowl with the sun-dried tomatoes and bread and then pour over the oil dressing. Toss together well.

Arrange the salad on a serving dish, top with the hard-boiled eggs, and finish with a final drizzle of olive oil.

TROFIE CON LE PUNTARELLE
Trofie pasta with puntarelle

Puntarelle are the sprouts of a special variety of Catalonian chicory. Like chicory, they have a pleasant, slightly bitter taste, and can be turned into a lovely simple pasta dish when in season. This recipe uses the outer leaves and stems, and you can use the crunchy inner shoots to make a salad (see page 95).

SERVES 4

14 oz (400 g) puntarelle leaves and stems, roughly chopped
11 oz (320 g) trofie pasta
3 tbsp extra virgin olive oil
2 garlic cloves, finely sliced
½ red chile, finely sliced
5 anchovy fillets
3 tsp capers
sea salt
grated Parmesan, to finish (optional)

Bring a pot of salted water to a boil and cook the *puntarelle* for about 2 minutes, then lift out with tongs and set aside. In the same pot, cook the *trofie* pasta until al dente, then drain, reserving a little of the pasta water.

Meanwhile, heat the olive oil in a large frying pan over medium heat and sweat the garlic, chile, anchovy fillets, and capers. Add the *puntarelle* and stir-fry over high heat, adding a couple of tablespoons of the pasta water, for about 5 minutes until tender.

Add the pasta to the *puntarelle*, mixing well over high heat for about a minute to combine thoroughly. Remove from the heat and serve immediately with some grated Parmesan, if you like.

SPINACH
SPINACI

Spinach is an ancient leaf vegetable that originated in Persia (today's Iran), thousands of years ago, and was first brought to Sicily and Spain by the Arabs, from where it eventually spread throughout the rest of Europe. It is said that Catherine de Medici loved spinach so much that she had to eat it every day, which explains why dishes containing spinach are often known as "Florentine."

Spinach is a popular vegetable the world over and Italy is no exception. Abundant in the spring, it is used in many dishes and prized for its taste and health benefits. When cooked, its earthy flavor and compact texture combines well with many ingredients—garlic, chile, anchovies, lemon, creamy cheeses and sauces, Parmesan, eggs, pancetta, mushrooms, walnuts, and so much more.

In the Italian kitchen, spinach is commonly combined with ricotta cheese to make the classic filling for ravioli, pasta bakes (see page 101), and *crespelle* (pancakes), and is also a must for the traditional Easter savory tart, *Torta Pasqualina*. Spinach is commonly added to soups, pasta, and risotto, as well as frittata, savory pies, soufflés, and *sformato*-type dishes. It is also used to make *gnudi*, a gnocchi-type dumpling (see page 102) and, very finely chopped, it can color fresh pasta dough. Simply sautéed in olive oil and garlic, it makes a delicious side dish, and small, young spinach leaves are perfect in salads, tossed in olive oil and lemon juice.

How to use spinach:

Buying and storing
Look for fresh, firm, dark green leaves without blemishes or signs of yellowing. Once home, it can be stored in the fridge for a couple of days.

Preparing
Spinach is quick to cook but the preparation can be a little time-consuming. Remove any tough stalks from larger leaves and then thoroughly wash the spinach. Blanch it in lots of boiling water for about 2 minutes until cooked through, then drain well. When cool enough, squeeze out the excess water with your hands, then roughly chop and use as required. Blanch small leaves for about 30 seconds or add to stews and soups at the end until they wilt.

You can also pick up ready-prepared bags of both large and baby spinach in supermarkets, as well as bags of frozen whole leaf or chopped spinach. Frozen spinach is available all year round in small portion blocks. It's so easy to just grab a couple of frozen portions and add them to a soup or stew, they cook through quickly. Or defrost them in the microwave.

Remember that, whatever weight your frozen spinach is, half of it will be water. This is also true when cooking fresh spinach. Spinach shrinks dramatically when cooked. Allow about 9 oz (250 g) raw spinach per person if serving as a side dish.

LASAGNE CON SPINACI
Spinach lasagne

This nourishing cheesy lasagne can be made using mostly pantry ingredients. I always keep a package of frozen spinach in my freezer as it's so handy to use in dishes like this, and so nutritious.

SERVES 4

1 lb 2 oz (500 g) frozen spinach
1½ tbsp extra virgin olive oil
2 garlic cloves, left whole and squashed
heaped 1 cup (250 g) ricotta
½ cup (50 g) grated Parmesan
10–12 dried lasagne sheets
1 x 4½ oz (125 g) ball of mozzarella cheese, drained and roughly chopped
sea salt and freshly ground black pepper

For the béchamel
3 tbsp butter
⅓ cup (40 g) all-purpose flour
2 cups (500 ml) milk
¼ cup (25 g) grated Parmesan
sea salt and freshly ground black pepper

Preheat the oven to 400°F (200°C).

Defrost the spinach, then squeeze out the excess liquid with your hands and set aside.

Heat the olive oil in a frying pan over medium heat and sweat the garlic for a minute, then add the spinach, turn up the heat, and stir-fry for a couple of minutes. Remove from the heat, discard the garlic cloves, and set aside to cool.

Now make the béchamel. In a saucepan, melt the butter over low heat, then take off the heat and whisk in the flour until you have a smooth paste. Gradually whisk in the milk, then return to the heat, whisking all the time, until the sauce begins to thicken slightly. Remove from the heat, season with salt and pepper, and stir in the grated Parmesan.

In a bowl, combine the cooled spinach with the ricotta and half the Parmesan and season to taste.

Line a baking dish (approx. 7 in x 9½ in/18 cm x 24 cm) with a little of the béchamel, followed by a couple of lasagne sheets, then a thin layer of the spinach mixture, and then a layer béchamel. Scatter some mozzarella on top and sprinkle with Parmesan, then cover with lasagne sheets. Continue making layers like these until you have finished up all the ingredients, ending with béchamel and a sprinkle of Parmesan.

Cover with foil and bake in the oven for 20 minutes, then remove the foil and bake for a further 20 minutes, until golden and bubbly on top.

Remove from the oven, leave to rest for at least 5 minutes, then slice and serve.

GNOCCHI DI SPINACI
Spinach gnocchi

This delicious potato-less gnocchi is made with the classic combination of spinach and ricotta. It is simple to prepare, just remember to squeeze out the excess liquid from the cooked spinach before mixing with the rest of the ingredients. Serve with tomato sauce for a hearty meal.

SERVES 4

9 oz (250 g) frozen spinach
heaped 1 cup (250 g) ricotta
1 egg
6 tbsp grated Parmesan, plus extra for sprinkling
pinch of grated nutmeg
sea salt
2 cups (250 g) "00" flour, plus extra for dusting

For the tomato sauce
2 tbsp extra virgin olive oil
2 garlic cloves, finely sliced
1 x 14 oz (400 g) can chopped tomatoes
sea salt

First make the tomato sauce. Heat the olive oil in a heavy-based sauté pan over medium heat and sweat the garlic for a minute or so, then add the tomatoes with a little water (rinsed from the can) and a little salt. Cover with a lid and cook over medium-low heat for about 25 minutes.

Meanwhile, make the gnocchi. Bring a pot of salted water to a boil and cook the frozen spinach for about 5 minutes until defrosted and cooked through. Drain well, squeezing out the excess liquid with your hands, then place on a chopping board and finely chop.

Place the spinach in a large bowl with the ricotta, egg, Parmesan, nutmeg, and a little salt, and gradually add in the flour. Mix well until you obtain a smooth, soft dough.

On a lightly floured work surface, roll the dough out into a long sausage shape. Using a sharp knife, cut into 1 in (2.5 cm) lengths. Continue doing this until all the dough has been used up.

Bring a large pot of salted water to a boil and drop the gnocchi into the water in batches, simmering for a minute or so until they rise to the top.

Using a slotted spoon or a spider strainer, lift the gnocchi out of the water and transfer to a dish. Pour over the tomato sauce and gently mix. Serve immediately with a sprinkling of grated Parmesan, if you like.

SFORMATO DI SPINACI
Cheesy *spinach* "terrine"

This savory spinach loaf cake makes a lovely main dish, served with either boiled new potato salad or bread and perhaps a mixed or arugula salad. Very easy to prepare, you can make it in advance and enjoy it both hot or cold. You can store it in the fridge and just cut a slice or two whenever you like.

SERVES 8

3 eggs
scant ½ cup (100 ml) milk
scant ½ cup (100 ml) sunflower oil
scant ½ cup (100 ml) extra virgin olive oil
1½ cups (180 g) all-purpose flour, sifted
1¾ tsp baking powder
handful of basil leaves, roughly torn
1 lb (450 g) frozen spinach, defrosted
5¼ oz (150 g) provolone dolce cheese, grated
1 x 4½ oz (125 g) ball of mozzarella cheese, drained and roughly chopped
sea salt and freshly ground black pepper

Preheat the oven to 400°F (200°C) and line a 9 in x 5½ in (900 g) loaf pan with parchment paper.

Beat the eggs in a large bowl, then add the milk, both oils, and a little salt and pepper. Whisk in the flour and baking powder, then add the basil leaves, spinach, provolone, and mozzarella and stir to combine.

Pour the mixture evenly into the prepared pan and bake in the oven for 50 minutes until risen and golden.

Remove from the oven, leave to rest for 5 minutes, then turn out, slice, and serve.

Green Vegetables

Peppers
Swiss Chard
Tomatoes

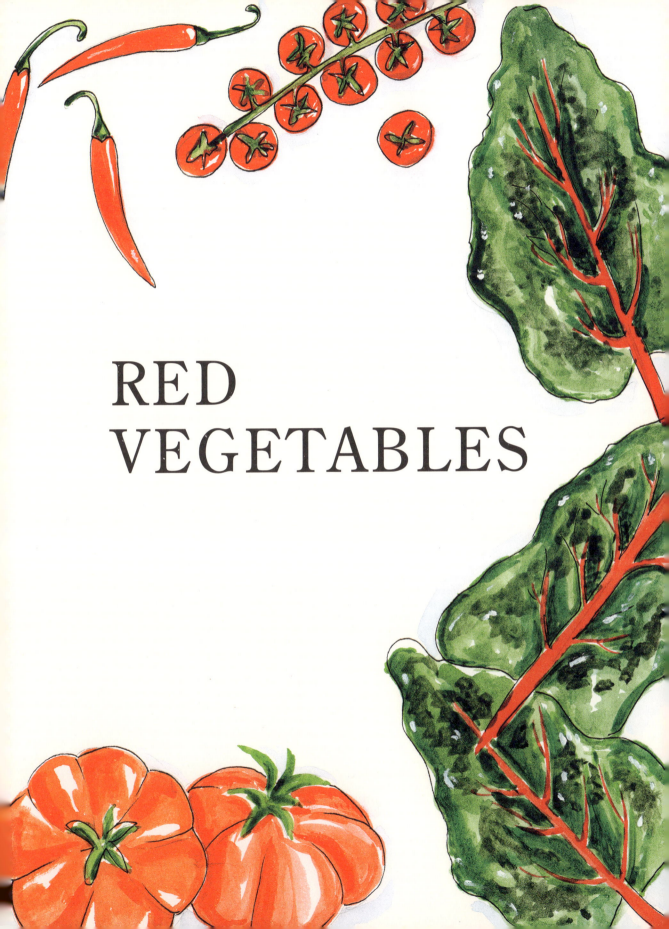

RED VEGETABLES

PEPPERS
PEPERONI

In vibrant colors of red, yellow, orange, and green, not many vegetables shout "Mediterranean sun" as loudly as peppers, and this sun-kissed capsicum is much loved in Italy. Originating in South America and the Caribbean, they are thought to have been introduced to Europe by Christopher Columbus, and the name *peperoni* or "peppers" in English was given at the time to anything that tasted pungent. *Pepe,* in Italian, means pepper, so the word *peperoni* translates as "large pepper." They belong to the Capsicum family, along with chiles. However, most pepper varieties are much larger than chiles and have a sweet taste, without the heat that is so characteristic of chiles. Abundant in the summer, they are commonly preserved in Italy so their flavors can be enjoyed all year round.

Peppers are grown throughout Italy and come in many shapes and sizes, with a huge variety of tastes and textures. *Peperone di Carmagnola, di Cuneo,* and *Quadrato d'Asti* are large, square-shaped peppers from Piemonte, with a thick "meaty" flesh. These really are no match for the thin-skinned greenhouse-grown bell peppers that we often find in supermarkets. Also from Piemonte, the *Lungo* or *Corno di Bue* are long, slim, and horn-like in shape with a thinner flesh. The *Peperone di Pontecorvo* from Rome is a sweet red pepper and a similar long shape. The *Peperone di Senise,* from rural Basilicata, are sun-dried and known as *peperoni cruschi,* and these dried peppers are used in many local dishes and impart a smoky flavor. In the Naples area, *Papaccelle Napoletane* are small squashed peppers with a sweet flavor and are used for preserving. They are a favorite in the classic Christmas salad *Insalata di Rinforzo.* The sweet-tasting *Friggitelli* or *Friarielli* are small, thin, green peppers, much-loved by Neapolitans, who fry them whole with olive oil and garlic.

Italians use peppers in a multitude of dishes. They are often stuffed with ground meat or vegetarian ingredients, like leftover stale bread, cheese, olives, and capers (see page 113). Peppers are also used in pasta (see page 114) and risotto dishes, or simply fried and served with meat or in a frittata. They can also be made into *Peperonata* (see page 110), a stew of mixed peppers and tomato, but one of my favorite ways is to cook them *agrodolce,* with sweet and sour flavors. This makes an excellent antipasto or can be served alongside meat or fish or simply eaten with bread as a snack.

Raw peppers are not that popular in Italy. They are sometimes added to salads, but Italians prefer them cooked. Cooked peppers are delicious blended to a creamy consistency and added to freshly cooked pasta or as a topping for bruschetta. Roasting peppers enhances the flavor further and Italians often do this and then combine them with olive oil, garlic, salt, and parsley, and serve them as a salad or stirred through pasta dishes. Grilled peppers are common in a mixed grilled vegetable platter.

Peperoncino, chile peppers, are smaller, with a fiery pungent taste, and are used in an entirely different way. Small amounts are used to flavor dishes and they are often added to *soffritto* or sautéed with olive oil and garlic. In Calabria, in southern Italy, red chiles are popular in a lot of dishes and, even added to local cured meats, like *soppressata* and the spreadable salami *'nduja*. Chiles are consumed fresh and dried, or preserved in jars of oil.

How to use peppers:

Buying and storing
Red, yellow, and orange peppers are the sweetest. The green ones are unripe red peppers and have a bitter taste. However, once cooked, they can be sweet enough.

Look for ones that are bright in color, plump, firm, and smooth. Avoid any with soft patches or wrinkles, as this means they are deteriorating. Once home, store in the salad drawer of the fridge for up to about a week.

Preparing
When slicing raw peppers, you need to remove the pith and seeds.

Roasting
Preheat the oven to its highest setting (about 460°F/240°C). Place the whole peppers on a baking sheet and roast for 40–50 minutes, depending on size, until soft and charred in places. Remove from the oven and leave until cool enough to handle. Remove the skin (this should come off easily), discard the pith and seeds inside, then finely chop the flesh and use according to your recipe.

Preserving
Use the sweeter red and yellow peppers. Cut them in half, remove the pith and seeds, then slice into thin strips. Place in a container, sprinkle with salt, cover with parchment paper, and place a weight over the top, then leave for 1–2 hours, after which time they will have exuded a lot of liquid. Take the peppers in your hands and squeeze out the excess liquid, then place back in a clean container, cover with white wine vinegar, and leave again for about 1 hour. Drain the peppers again, squeezing out the excess liquid with your hands, before placing them in a bowl with sliced garlic, finely sliced chile, a little dried oregano, and mild olive oil. Mix well together, then place in sterilized jars, secure tightly with a lid and leave in the fridge for a couple of days before using.

PEPERONATA
Stewed *peppers*

You can make this classic Italian pepper stew with raw peppers, however, the taste of chargrilled peppers gives extra flavor and depth. It's delicious to make during the summer months when peppers are plentiful and at their best. Serve with lots of rustic bread to mop up the sauce.

SERVES 4

1 lb 9 oz (700 g) mixed red and yellow peppers
3 tbsp extra virgin olive oil
2 onions, finely sliced
2 garlic cloves, squashed and left whole
2 x 14 oz (400 g) cans chopped tomatoes
handful of whole basil leaves, to garnish
sea salt

Place the whole peppers on a hot grill pan or under a hot broiler and cook, turning from time to time, until the skin blackens.

Remove from the heat and, with the help of a kitchen towel so you don't burn your fingers, carefully remove the skin, pith, and seeds—this is best done while the peppers are still hot. Slice the flesh into strips and set aside.

Heat the olive oil in a heavy-based pot over medium heat and sweat the onions and garlic for a couple of minutes until softened. Add the canned tomatoes with a little salt, then cover with a lid and cook over low-medium heat for about 15 minutes. Add the peppers and continue to cook over low heat, partially covered with a lid, for 45 minutes.

Garnish with the basil leaves then serve hot with lots of crusty, rustic bread.

PEPERONI ALLA MOLLICA
Peppers with breadcrumbs

This *cucina povera* recipe from Sicily uses up leftover bread, which enriches the peppers and makes the dish go further. It can be enjoyed hot or cold, as a side or together with cured meats and cheese as an antipasto or light lunch.

SERVES 4 AS A SIDE DISH OR ANTIPASTO

1 lb 5 oz (600 g) mixed red and yellow peppers
3 tbsp extra virgin olive oil
1¾ oz (50 g) stale bread, roughly chopped
1 garlic clove, finely diced
1 tsp capers
3 tbsp grated pecorino cheese
pinch of dried oregano
sea salt

Cut the peppers in half lengthways, discard the seeds and the white pith, and slice into thick strips.

Heat the olive oil in a frying pan over high heat and stir-fry the peppers for a minute. Add a little salt, reduce the heat to medium, and cover with a lid, then continue to cook for about 15 minutes, turning the peppers over from time to time, until they have softened.

Meanwhile, place the bread, garlic, capers, pecorino, and oregano in a food processor and pulse until the bread is nice and crumbly. Sprinkle the mixture over the peppers, cover with a lid, and cook over medium heat for a couple of minutes.

Remove the lid, increase the heat, and stir-fry for a further couple of minutes until the bread is nicely golden, then serve straight away.

PEPERONI RIPIENI
Filled *peppers*

In Italy, we enjoy peppers when they are plentiful, all through the summer, and fill them with whatever ingredients we have on hand. This recipe also uses other seasonal vegetables—zucchinis, tomatoes, and olives, with a little smoky scamorza, but you could use eggplants instead of zucchinis or simply tomatoes and whatever cheese you have on hand. This dish can be made in advance and heated up when required or enjoyed cold.

SERVES 4–5

3 tbsp extra virgin olive oil, plus extra for drizzling
4 garlic cloves, squashed and left whole
2 zucchinis (approx. 15 oz/420 g), cut into small cubes
6¼ oz (180 g) baby plum tomatoes, cut in half
12 pitted black olives
1½ oz (40 g) bread, finely chopped
8 basil leaves
4¼ oz (120 g) scamorza cheese, finely chopped
4 red or yellow peppers
sea salt and freshly ground black pepper

Preheat the oven to 400°F (200°C).

Heat the olive oil in a frying pan over medium heat and sweat the garlic cloves for a minute. Add the zucchinis and stir-fry for about 10 minutes until golden, then transfer to a plate with a slotted spoon and discard the garlic cloves. Set aside.

In the same pan, add the tomatoes and olives and stir-fry over medium heat for a couple of minutes. Remove from the heat and combine with the zucchinis, bread, basil leaves, and three-quarters of the scamorza.

Slice the peppers in half lengthways and remove and discard the seeds and white pith.

Drizzle a little olive oil inside each pepper half and divide the zucchini mixture among them. Drizzle a little more olive oil in a baking dish large enough to accommodate all the peppers and arrange the filled peppers inside, filled-side up. Scatter the remaining scamorza cheese over the peppers and finish with a final drizzle of olive oil. Cover with foil and bake in the oven for 40 minutes, then remove the foil and continue to bake for a further 20–30 minutes, until the peppers are cooked through. Serve immediately or cool, then chill in the fridge until required.

PENNE CON CREMA DI PEPERONI ARROSTITI

Penne with creamy roasted *pepper* sauce

If you like the taste of roasted peppers, this recipe is for you as they combine perfectly with penne pasta. If you are in a hurry, you can skip the roasting and simply sauté the peppers; see tip below.

SERVES 4

- 1 lb 2 oz (500 g) mixed red and yellow peppers
- 3 tbsp extra virgin olive oil
- 2 garlic cloves, squashed and left whole
- ½ handful of basil leaves and stalks
- ½ cup (50 g) grated Parmesan
- 11 oz (320 g) penne rigate
- sea salt and freshly ground black pepper

Preheat the oven to 450°F (240°C).

Place the whole peppers in a roasting pan and roast for about 45 minutes, until the skin has blackened and the peppers have softened.

Remove from the oven and, with the help of a kitchen towel so you don't burn your fingers, carefully remove the skin, pith, and seeds—this is best done while the peppers are still hot. Roughly slice the flesh and set aside.

Heat the olive oil in a heavy-based pot over medium heat and sweat the garlic and basil stalks for about a minute. Add the sliced peppers and stir-fry for 5 minutes so the flavors infuse nicely. Remove from the heat, discard the garlic, then transfer to a blender. Add the basil leaves and Parmesan and blend until smooth.

Meanwhile, bring a large pot of salted water to a boil and cook the penne until al dente, then drain and combine with the creamy pepper sauce. Serve immediately with extra Parmesan, basil leaves, and some black pepper.

TIP

If you're short on time, you can skip roasting the peppers and simply sauté them, thinly sliced, in the pot with the garlic for about 20 minutes, until they are soft and cooked through.

SWISS CHARD
BIETOLE

Bietole, sometimes referred to as *coste* in Italy, is what we know as Swiss chard. It is not clear why it is known as this, as it originated on the sandy banks of the southern Mediterranean, rather than Switzerland. It is probably one of the oldest members of the beet family (*Beta Vulgaris*) and has been in existence for centuries. The Ancient Romans prized it for culinary as well as medicinal purposes.

Chard has large and fleshy green leaves with white ribs and thick white stalks that have a similar texture to celery. The leaves tend to be used in the same way as spinach and the stalks provide a nice contrasting crunch. Some varieties have red ribs and vibrantly colored stalks in red, orange, yellow, and purple, and this is known as rainbow chard.

Chard grows all over Italy and is available from about May through to November. It is packed with nutrients, including vitamins and antioxidants and is apparently excellent for improving digestion.

Some recipes call for just the leaves to be used; for example, in ravioli where a smooth filling is required. However, the stalks are never discarded and are sliced into chunks and sautéed in olive oil or butter and served as a side dish.

Like spinach, Swiss chard's earthy taste combines well with lots of flavors, like garlic, chile, anchovies, olives, mushrooms, pancetta, béchamel sauces, Parmesan, eggs, legumes, beans, and so much more. It can be added to vegetable soups, pasta dishes, frittatas (see page 123), bean stews, and savory pies and tarts. In Lucca in Tuscany, they combine chard with raisins, walnuts, and candied citrus peel to make a traditional sweet tart, which is delicious (see page 120).

How to use chard:

Buying and storing
Look for healthy bright green leaves that are unblemished and not yellowing or withered. The stems should be crisp, firm, and not droopy. At home, chard can be stored in the fridge for a couple of days.

Preparing
First wash, then cut the stalks from the leaves, including as much of the rib as you can. If you are cooking both together, remember to cook the stalks first, before adding the leaves.

Here is a quick and simple way to cook chard. The combination of the crunchy stalks and walnuts combines perfectly with the soft texture of the leaves and it makes a delicious side dish.

Roughly chop the chard stalks into chunks and roughly chop the leaves. Melt some butter in a frying pan, add the stalks, season with salt and pepper, and then sauté for a couple of minutes. Add a splash of hot water, cover with a lid, and cook over medium heat for about 10 minutes, stirring now and again. Add the green leaves, cover with the lid and continue to cook for a further 5 minutes. Stir in a handful of chopped walnuts and some grated Parmesan, then remove from the heat and serve.

TORTA DOLCE DI BIETOLE
Sweet *chard* tart

This traditional sweet tart from Lucca in Tuscany has ancient origins and turns local greens into something rather special. Known locally as *torta coi becchi*, it is delicious eaten at breakfast or for afternoon tea. It is quite filling so a slice will keep you going for a while.

SERVES 6–8

3 oz (80 g) rustic bread
⅔ cup (150 ml) milk
¼ cup (45 g) raisins
2 tbsp rum
11 oz (320 g) rainbow or Swiss chard
1½ tbsp butter
2 eggs
scant ½ cup (80 g) sugar, any type
¼ cup (50 g) candied citrus peel
¼ cup (30 g) roughly chopped walnuts
zest of 1 lemon
pinch of ground cinnamon
pinch of grated nutmeg
13 oz (375 g) ready-made shortcrust pastry, thawed if frozen
all-purpose flour, for dusting
confectioners' sugar, for dusting
sea salt

Preheat the oven to 350°F (180°C). Break up the bread into pieces, place in a bowl, and soak in the milk to soften. In another bowl, soak the raisins in the rum.

Chop the chard stalks into small pieces and place in a pot of salted water, together with the chard leaves. Bring to a boil and cook for 5–6 minutes until tender. Drain well, then squeeze out the leaves with your hands to remove the excess liquid. Transfer to a chopping board and finely chop the leaves

Melt the butter in a frying pan over medium heat, add the chard (stems and leaves), and sweat for about 5 minutes until the butter has been absorbed.

Lightly beat the eggs with the sugar until creamy.

In a large bowl, combine the chard, softened bread, rum-soaked raisins, candied citrus peel, walnuts, lemon zest, cinnamon, nutmeg, and egg mixture.

Roll out the pastry on a lightly floured work surface to a thickness of about ¼ in (5 mm) and line the base and sides of an 8½ in (22 cm) round pie dish with it. Fill with the chard mixture.

Roll out the excess pastry again, cut out strips, and place in a lattice design over the mixture. Bake in the oven for about 50 minutes.

Remove from the oven, leave to cool, then dust with confectioners' sugar before slicing and serving.

FRITTATA DI BIETOLE ALLA LIGURE
Ligurian-style rainbow *chard* frittata

This Ligurian-style frittata includes sweet raisins and crunchy pine nuts, which complement the chard. I love the colors of rainbow chard but, if you can't find it, use the white-stemmed variety or spinach instead. Served with rustic bread and a salad, this makes an easy meal. You can also enjoy the frittata cold in a *panino* (sandwich) for a packed lunch or picnic.

SERVES 4

1 bunch of rainbow chard, about 14 oz (400 g) in total
2 tbsp extra virgin olive oil
1 garlic clove, left whole and squashed
2 anchovy fillets
leaves of 1 thyme sprig
1½ tbsp raisins, soaked in a little warm water
1½ tbsp pine nuts
6 eggs
2½ tbsp grated Parmesan
red onion, finely sliced, to garnish
sea salt and freshly ground black pepper

Discard the hard ends of the chard stem and finely slice the rest of the stalks and the leaves.

Heat the olive oil in a medium-large frying pan over medium heat and sweat the garlic, anchovy fillets, and thyme leaves for a minute or so until the anchovy fillets have dissolved. Discard the garlic.

Add the chard and stir-fry over medium-high heat for a minute or so to allow the chard to flavor. Add the softened raisins and pine nuts, then lower the heat, cover with a lid, and cook for about 5 minutes until the chard is tender.

Remove the lid, turn up the heat, and cook off any excess liquid.

Meanwhile, lightly beat the eggs in a bowl with a little salt and pepper and the grated Parmesan. Pour the egg mixture over the chard and cook in the pan like an omelet. You can either flip the frittata over or you could place it under a hot broiler until it cooks and turns golden brown.

Remove from the heat and garnish with some red onion before slicing and serving.

CRESCIONE ROMAGNOLO
Filled *flatbread* from Emilia Romangna

This is Emilia Romagna's answer to the Neapolitan calzone, but is much quicker to make and cook. It's a common street-food snack, especially along the coastal areas, and was traditionally made with local greens. I have opted for Swiss chard, but you could also use spinach, spring greens, and any leftover cheese and/or cured meats you may have in the fridge. Enjoy as a snack or with a tomato salad for a meal at any time.

MAKES 6–8

For the dough
2 cups (250 g) "00" flour, plus extra for dusting
pinch of baking soda
pinch of sea salt
scant ½ cup (100 ml) water
2¼ tbsp extra virgin olive oil

For the filling
1 lb 4 oz (550 g) Swiss chard
2 tbsp extra virgin olive oil
½ onion, finely chopped
¼ cup (25 g) grated pecorino cheese
sea salt and freshly ground black pepper

First make the dough. In a large bowl, combine the flour, baking soda, and salt, then gradually add the water and olive oil and work into a dough with your hands. Knead for about 10 minutes, then form into a ball and leave to rest at room temperature for about 30 minutes.

Meanwhile, finely chop the stems of the chard and roughly chop the leaves.

Heat the olive oil in a frying pan over medium heat and sweat the onion until softened. Stir in the chard stems and continue to sweat until the stems begin to soften. Stir in the chard leaves and season with a little salt and pepper, then reduce the heat, cover with a lid, and cook for about 15 minutes until tender. Remove from the heat, stir in the grated pecorino and set aside.

Divide the dough into 6–8 pieces, each weighing approx. 2¼ oz (65 g). Lightly dust a work surface with flour and roll out each piece as thinly as you can (about 1 mm thick) into a roughly round shape (about 6 in/15 cm in diameter). Cover with a cloth to avoid them drying out.

Place a good amount of filling on one half of each circle, leaving a border of about ¼ in (5 mm) around the edge. Brush water over the dough and fold like a calzone, pressing down and sealing well to ensure none of the filling can escape. Using a fork, make indentations to secure thoroughly.

Heat a heavy-based, non-stick pan over high-medium heat and cook the *crescioni* on each side until golden brown. Depending on how big your pan is, you will probably have to do this in batches, keeping the *crescioni* warm until they are all cooked. Serve immediately.

TIP
These are best eaten hot, but you can make them in advance and enjoy cold.

TOMATOES
Pomodori

Tomatoes are integral to Italian cooking. They form the basis of so many sauces and dishes and are also such a joy to eat raw in salads that the tomato really is king of the kitchen!

Native to Central and South America, the tomato was introduced to Italy around the sixteenth century but took another couple of centuries to be completely accepted and enjoyed. Belonging to the nightshade family, it was first viewed with much suspicion and thought to be poisonous. However, bakers in Naples began putting tomatoes on their flatbreads for extra nutrition to feed the poor and it was so well received that even the aristocracy were drawn in (which is probably how today's pizza originated).

The original tomato was a golden yellow color, hence the Italian name *pomodoro*, meaning golden apple. Over time, it evolved into the red color we know and love and associate with all the sauces and ragùs in Italian cooking.

Although most commercial tomato production is in Puglia, Campania, and Emilia Romagna, most regions in Italy grow tomatoes and each one boasts its own different varieties and specialties. The large beef tomato, often known in Italy as *Cuore di Bue,* is used in salads, as well as to make tomato sauces. In Sicily, *Ciliegino di Pachino* is a sweet cherry tomato. *Pomodorino del Piennolo* from the Vesuvius area is a small, sweet baby plum tomato, cut from the vine and hung in bunches, where they can last for months. Sardinia produces a red-green variety, known as *Pomodoro di Camone,* with a fresh flavor and firm, crunchy texture that is perfect for salads. The popular plum-shaped flavorful *Roma* is used in sauces, and one of the best-loved varieties is the *San Marzano,* grown in the lush volcanic soils of Vesuvius, which produces a long, thin plum tomato with fewer seeds, a lower water content, and a sweet rich flavor. It is the favorite for using in rich tomato sauces but is also delicious to enjoy raw in a salad.

Tomatoes are so versatile and, as well as being the hero of myriad sauces, they are perfect for stuffing (see page 133), made into soups like *Pappa al Pomodoro,* or *Panzanella* bread salad, or added to pasta, risotto dishes, stews, savory tarts, frittatas, pizzas, bruschetta, and so much more (see my recipe for sorbet on page 136). They are delicious roasted with garlic and basil and served with pasta, or simply enjoyed with bread for mopping up all the delicious juices.

One of my favorite quick meals is to lightly sauté some ripe baby tomatoes with olive oil and garlic and toss through some freshly cooked spaghetti (see page 130). It takes no time to cook and provides a satisfying meal every time.

When I was growing up in Italy, the tomato harvest at the end of summer was always a busy time, as preparations got underway to preserve as many tomatoes in as many ways as possible to last us through the winter. Plum tomatoes were quartered and, together with the odd basil leaf, pushed into thick brown beer bottles, which had been sterilized and were later placed in our pantry; this was our equivalent to canned plum tomatoes. It was a lengthy process but one that no one could afford not to do.

Tomatoes were also made into passata, or sun-dried, or turned into a thick concentrated paste, known as *estratto*, which became dark red in color and just a teaspoon was enough to flavor dishes. A lot of hard work went into this annual ritual, but it was necessary to ensure we had a good supply of different types to satisfy all our cooking requirements through the winter ahead. Every time we opened a bottle of tomatoes, the taste and memories of summer would come flooding back, warming us on bleak winter days. Even though no longer necessary, some people in Italy still do this today and trays of sliced tomatoes can often be seen on balconies and roof terraces, soaking up the hot summer sun. When we get hot sunny days in the UK, I do the same, and the taste is quite something and so different from the commercially produced sun-dried tomatoes you find on supermarket shelves.

We are lucky to have such an array of preserved tomatoes on the market today—canned whole plum, chopped, cherry tomatoes, jars of passata, tubes of paste, sun-dried, sun-blushed. Passata is strained tomato pulp, which is good for when you want a smooth texture, like tomato soup. Tomato paste is used in small quantities to enrich sauces, and sun-dried tomatoes can liven up dishes or sandwiches, or served as part of an antipasto with cured meats and cheese.

Although we can get all sorts of tomatoes all year round now, summer is still the best time of year for the freshest and best local varieties. This is the time to really make the most of the different types and, if you do happen to buy too many, simply preserve them in sterilized bottles or jars, as that way they will last you a long time. A salad of perfectly ripe, sweet-smelling tomatoes is a joy, simply sprinkled with a little salt and dried oregano or basil and drizzled with olive oil—it's summer on a plate!

How to use *tomatoes*:

Storing
Never store tomatoes in the fridge as the cold destroys their flavor. Keep them in a bowl at room temperature. If you've bought ripe tomatoes, they will last a few days; unripe ones at least a week.

Preparing
The simplest way to peel tomatoes is to make a small cross in the tops with a sharp knife and then place in boiling water for about a minute. When drained, the skin should come off easily. To deseed, simply cut in half and scoop out the seeds with a teaspoon.

SALSA VELOCE DI POMODORINI
Quick *tomato* sauce

This is one of my favorite pasta sauces and a go-to when I don't have much time to cook. It's quick, simple and, tossed through some freshly cooked pasta, makes a satisfying meal every time.

SERVES 4

¼ cup (60 ml) extra virgin olive oil
3 garlic cloves, finely sliced
½ red chile, finely chopped
1 lb 5 oz (600 g) baby plum or cherry tomatoes, halved or quartered depending on size
handful of basil leaves, roughly torn
sea salt

Heat the olive oil in a heavy-based pot over medium heat and sweat the garlic and chile for a minute.

Increase the heat, add the tomatoes with a little salt, and stir-fry over high heat for about 3 minutes, until softened but not too mushy (the tomatoes should still be intact).

Remove the pot from the heat, add the basil, and use according to your recipe.

POMODORI RIPIENI DI PASTA
Stuffed *tomatoes*

This is a great way of making the most out of delicious, sun-ripened, summer tomatoes. I use the large vine tomatoes, but you could use beef tomatoes or any type that are large. Stuffing them with pasta makes a very satisfying meal, perhaps with a green salad on the side. I like to mix the pasta with my favorite quick tomato sauce (see page 130), but you could make this recipe with any cooked leftover pasta dish you have on hand—a Bolognese or cheesy pasta would be great. However, it needs to be short-shaped pasta to fit inside the tomatoes.

MAKES 6

6 large vine tomatoes
3 oz (80 g) short pasta shapes, e.g. macaroni, mezzi rigatoni, pennette, farfalle, spirali
½ quantity of Quick Tomato Sauce (see page 130)
3 tbsp (20 g) grated Parmesan
extra virgin olive oil, for greasing and drizzling
approx. 1 tbsp dried breadcrumbs
½ handful of basil leaves
sea salt

Preheat the oven to 400°F (200°C).

Slice off the tops of the tomatoes and reserve them. Using a small teaspoon, carefully scoop out the seeds and insides in order to obtain an empty tomato shell. Do this over a sieve placed over a bowl so you can discard the seeds but keep the juices to add to the sauce.

Sprinkle salt inside the tomatoes, then place them upside down on a dish and leave them to exude as much liquid as possible while you prepare the rest of the ingredients.

Bring a large pot of salted water to a boil and cook the pasta until al dente, then drain.

Meanwhile, ready your tomato sauce. When adding the tomatoes, don't forget to add the juices from the large tomatoes.

Drain the pasta and mix well with the sauce, then stir in the Parmesan. Stuff the tomatoes with this mixture.

Lightly grease a baking dish with a little olive oil and arrange the tomatoes inside. Sprinkle with breadcrumbs, place the tops on the tomatoes, and drizzle with a little more oil. Cover with foil and bake in the oven for 25 minutes, then remove the foil and bake for a further 5 minutes, until the tomatoes have softened.

Garnish with some extra Parmesan and basil leaves before serving.

CAPRESE AL FORNO
Baked caprese "salad"

This is a twist on the traditional *caprese* salad that is loved so much in Italy, especially during the summer when tomatoes are at their best. This baked version could be mistaken for a "cheater's" pizza and makes a nice snack or light lunch. Try to get the hard mozzarella in blocks, it doesn't exude liquid like the traditional mozzarella balls and is perfect for this recipe as it doesn't make the bread soggy. However, if you can't find the hard type, then the soft mozzarella balls will do, but make sure you drain it really well and pat dry using paper towels before use.

SERVES 4

8 slices of rustic bread (5½–7 oz/ 150 g–200 g in total)
approx. 2 tbsp extra virgin olive oil, plus extra for drizzling
10½ oz (300 g) hard, low-moisture mozzarella, cut into 16 slices
approx. 2 tsp dried oregano
handful of basil leaves
1 large beef tomato (approx. 10½ oz/300 g), cut into 16 slices
8–10 pitted green olives, roughly chopped
sea salt and freshly ground black pepper

Preheat the oven to 250°F (120°C).

Place the slices of bread on a baking sheet and bake in the oven for about 20 minutes to allow the bread to dry out and crisp up a bit, then set aside.

Increase the oven temperature to 400°F (200°C).

Drizzle the bread slices with a little olive oil, then place 2 mozzarella slices on top of each, sprinkle with a little dried oregano, season with salt and pepper, and then add 2–3 basil leaves.

Top with the tomato slices—if your slices are not large enough, use a couple to cover the mozzarella. Scatter the chopped olives on top with more oregano and salt and pepper and finish with a drizzle of olive oil.

Bake in the oven for 12–15 minutes, until the mozzarella has melted.

Remove from the oven, drizzle with a little extra olive oil, and garnish with basil leaves before serving.

SORBETTO AL POMODORO
Tomato sorbet

When tomatoes are in abundance and at their best towards the end of summer, this sorbet is a winner. It can be served as a refreshing appetizer, with mozzarella skewers, or at the end of a meal or as a palate cleanser in between courses. The slight hint of chile gives it a nice kick and the tomato and basil are a perfect combination.

SERVES 6–8

1 lb 5 oz (600 g) large vine tomatoes
juice of 1 lemon
1 cup (200 g) white sugar
4 slices of red chile, plus extra to garnish
12 basil leaves

Place a clean, empty plastic container in the freezer (unless you have an ice-cream machine).

Using a sharp knife, make a small cross-like incision on the base of each tomato, then plunge them into boiling water for about a minute to soften the skins. Drain and carefully peel away the skins.

Cut the tomatoes in half and remove the seeds with the help of a teaspoon, catching the juices in a small bowl under a sieve. Discard the seeds.

Place the tomatoes with their juice in a blender. Add the lemon juice, sugar, chile slices, and basil leaves and blend until smooth.

If you are using an ice-cream machine, pour the mixture inside and churn. Otherwise, pour into the cold container, cover with a lid, and place in the freezer for about 30 minutes. Remove and stir well with a spoon, then replace in the freezer. Continue doing this every 30 minutes for 3–4 hours, until you obtain a sorbet-like consistency.

Remove from freezer about 5 minutes before serving, then scoop into bowls.

Belgian Endive
Carrots
Cauliflower
Mushrooms
Onions
Potatoes
Pumpkin/Squash

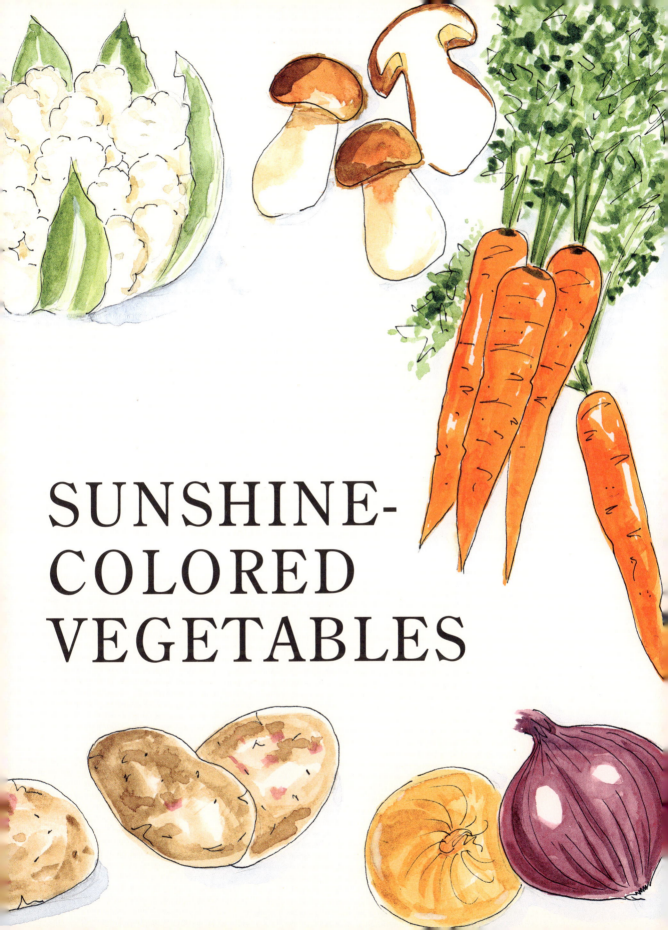

SUNSHINE-COLORED VEGETABLES

BELGIAN ENDIVES
ENDIVIA BELGA

As the name suggests, this vegetable from the chicory family originated in Belgium in the mid-1800's. It is a tightly packed, cylindrical head of white leaves with pale green tips and was originally called *witloof* (white leaf) by the Dutch. This labor-intensive crop wasn't really known in the rest of the world before the 1970s, when production processes became easier and higher quantities could be produced. This enabled it to be cultivated in other parts of Europe and it has become popular in the Italian kitchen—Italians love all types of slightly bitter-tasting chicory.

Belgian endive is a winter vegetable packed with vital nutrients and often consumed to promote digestive health. It is commonly used in salads (see page 155) but is also perfect for braising, roasting, or grilling, because when cooked, it loses the bitter taste completely. It is often baked with ham and a cheesy béchamel sauce, or stuffed with ground meat, and the leaves are often carefully taken apart and served like little "boats" with an aperitif, filled with salmon mousse or creamy blue cheese.

Indivia Scarola and *Indivia Riccia* are also part of the Italian chicory family and cooked in a similar way. Italians are very fond of braising the leaves with extra virgin olive oil and olives, adding them to soups, or stuffing the whole head with leftover stale bread, cheese, and other ingredients to make the vegetable go further. Unfortunately, these types of endives are not always readily available outside of Italy.

How to use Belgian endives:

Buying and storing
Look for tight, crisp leaves that are white to pale yellow in color. Avoid any with leaves that are wilting or brown at the edges. Store in the fridge, where it will keep fresh for a good few days.

Prepping and cooking
Remove the outer leaves of the endives if they feel tough, otherwise simply wash under cold running water and pat dry well with a cloth. Finely chop if using in a salad otherwise, if baking or stuffing, cut in half lengthways.

Belgian endives can be braised, baked, or roasted either whole or in halves. Simply warm some butter or extra virgin olive oil in a sauté pan, add the endives, and brown all over. Then add salted water or vegetable stock, cover with a lid, and leave to cook gently for about 30 minutes or so, until cooked through. They are also delicious cut in half and grilled, served with a dressing of extra virgin olive oil, mustard, honey, and chopped parsley or with a mixture of extra virgin olive oil, capers, and anchovies.

INSALATA DI ENDIVIA BELGA
Belgian endive salad

The slight bitterness of Belgian endives marries really well with the saltiness of both capers and anchovies. Ensure you use good-quality anchovies here as it will make all the difference. You could also add a few finely chopped sun-dried tomatoes for extra flavor, if you like. This makes a lovely accompaniment to many main dishes or simply enjoy on its own with some rustic bread.

SERVES 4–6

2 Belgian endives
2 tsp capers
6 anchovy fillets
½ handful of flat-leaf parsley
2 tbsp extra virgin olive oil

Using a sharp knife, slice the Belgian endives into very thin rounds, then place in a bowl.

Place the capers, anchovies, and parsley on a chopping board and finely chop together. Transfer to a small bowl, add the olive oil, and stir.

Pour the flavored oil over the endives and toss to coat well. Set aside to rest for about 20 minutes before serving, for all the flavors to infuse nicely.

Sunshine-Colored Vegetables

ENDIVIA BELGA RIPIENA
Filled *Belgian endives*

In my opinion, endive is an unfairly overlooked vegetable and, if you cook it, its slightly bitter taste disappears. If you want to reduce the cooking time slightly, don't combine the halves and simply drizzle them with oil and scatter with breadcrumbs. You could serve these as an appetizer or, as you are heating the oven, roast some potatoes alongside to create a complete meal.

SERVES 4

4 Belgian endives
3 tbsp extra virgin olive oil, plus extra for greasing and drizzling
2 small garlic cloves, finely chopped
7 oz (200 g) cremini mushrooms, finely chopped
leaves of 1 thyme sprig
2½ tbsp grated Parmesan
handful of flat-leaf parsley, very finely chopped
1 tbsp of dried breadcrumbs
sea salt and freshly ground black pepper

Preheat the oven to 400°F (200°C). Lightly grease a baking dish with olive oil.

Cut the endives in half lengthways and remove the hearts. Finely chop the hearts but keep the endive halves intact. Set aside.

Heat 2 tablespoons of olive oil in a frying pan over medium heat and sweat the garlic for a minute, then add the mushrooms and thyme and stir-fry for a couple of minutes. Transfer the cooked mushrooms to a plate and set aside.

Return the frying pan to the heat, add the remaining olive oil, and stir-fry the finely chopped endive hearts for 2–3 minutes, then lower the heat, cover with a lid, and gently cook for about 10 minutes until softened. Check from time to time and, if necessary, add a splash of water. Remove from the heat, combine with the mushrooms, Parmesan, and parsley, and season with salt and pepper to taste.

Fill the Belgian endive halves with this filling, then take two halves and tie them together with kitchen string. Place the filled endive inside the prepared baking dish. Season all over, drizzle with a little extra olive oil, and sprinkle with the breadcrumbs. Cover with foil and bake in the oven for 1 hour, then remove the foil and continue to bake for about 10 minutes, until golden brown.

Remove from the oven, leave to rest for a minute, then serve.

CARROTS
CAROTE

Carrots have a very important role in the Italian kitchen as they are one of the vegetables added to *soffritto* (a chopped-up blend of vegetables, herbs, and spices), which forms the base of many soups, sauces, and stews.

The carrot, as we know it today, originated from Afghanistan, but there is evidence that the Ancient Romans ate a root vegetable known as *pastinaca*, which was closely related to the carrot. In fact, *pastinaca* is the Italian word for parsnip, although in the Neapolitan dialect it is used to mean carrot! It is unsurprising as they are very similar—both impart a certain sweetness to dishes, and I have combined the two in my soup recipe on page 146.

Originally, carrots were grown for their aromatic leaves and seeds rather than for the root, which we enjoy today. Parsley, cilantro, fennel, dill, and cumin are part of the carrot family and are grown in the same way. The original carrots weren't always a vibrant orange color but rather white, yellow, red, and purple. These varieties are still grown today as heirloom carrots and available at some farmers' markets and specialty grocery stores. The story goes that the orange carrot was created by the Dutch, apparently in honor of their royal family, the House of Orange, by crossbreeding the red and yellow carrots. I'm not sure how true this is but we've been eating the orange variety for centuries now and it is the color we are most familiar with.

Carrots are grown all year round in Italy, from the north to the south, but the main regions are Abruzzo, Sicily, Puglia, Lazio, Veneto, Emilia Romagna, and Sardinia and each area specializes in different varieties, like the purple *Viola di Tiggiano* from Lecce in Puglia, or the sweet baby carrots of Ispica in Sicily.

I always have carrots at home as they are just so versatile and I couldn't imagine cooking without them. In my opinion, there is nothing more refreshing than a freshly grated carrot salad dressed with extra virgin olive oil and lemon juice, or the first new baby carrots in spring that are enjoyed in a *Pinzimonio*—a selection of fresh raw vegetables dipped into extra virgin olive oil.

In Italy, carrots are cooked whole when making a *Bollito di Manzo* or *Pollo* (boiled beef or chicken) and then served alongside the meat. Chopped up carrots are used in a wealth of soups, stews, ragùs, and sauces and always bring a tiny bit of natural sweetness to the dish. This sweetness also makes them ideal for cakes (see page 148) and other sweet treats likes scones and muffins. I've even come across a recipe for puréed carrot tiramisu!

When roasting meat, I always place a row of carrots, sliced in half lengthways, in the roasting pan underneath the meat as it not only prevents the meat from sticking, but it also gives you deliciously tender roasted carrots, flavored with the meat juices. Carrots are also wonderful puréed and combine deliciously with other root vegetables like celeriac (celery root), parsnips, or potatoes to make a creamy mash. They can be made into soufflé-type bakes (see page 151) or into fritters, as well as simply sautéed in a little extra virgin olive oil with chopped sage for a delicious side dish.

How to use *carrots*:

Buying and storing
Carrots come in all shapes and sizes and I really like the wonky imperfect ones that many shops now offer. I don't understand the need for perfection, as long as they taste good. Look for firm carrots without cracks or stringy bits at the bottom and, if the green leafy tops are still attached, make sure these are bright green and not yellowing.

Once home, cut off the green tops before storing as carrots lose their moisture through the tops and this may affect the quality of the carrots. Store the carrots in a cool, dry place in the kitchen or in the fridge. In the fridge, they will last a long time, but nutritionally they will lose value as well as taste. If you have old carrots that still look alright, they will still be edible, so use them in stocks and stews.

Preparing
You don't need to peel carrots as there's a lot of goodness in the peel; simply wash and use whole in your recipe.

CREMA DI CAROTE E PASTINACA ARROSTITE

Roasted *carrot* and parsnip soup

Roasting the vegetables really brings out their flavor and, in this simple recipe, the oven does all the work. Everything can even be done in one roasting pan. I really like the taste of parsnips so have added them, but you can leave them out and add more carrots, if you prefer. Serve with lightly toasted rustic bread.

SERVES 4

butter, for greasing
2 lb 4 oz (1 kg) carrots, peeled and cut into medium-sized chunks
2 medium parsnips, peeled and cut into medium-sized chunks
2 onions, cut into medium-sized chunks
2 medium potatoes, peeled and cut into medium-sized chunks
3 tbsp extra virgin olive oil, plus extra for drizzling
12 whole sage leaves
approx. 6$\frac{1}{3}$ cups (1.5 liters) hot vegetable stock
sea salt and freshly ground black pepper

Preheat the oven to 400°F (200°C).

Place all the vegetables in a roasting dish, drizzle with the olive oil, and season with a little salt and pepper and the sage leaves. Cover with foil and roast in the oven for 15 minutes, then discard the foil and continue to roast for a further 45 minutes until all the vegetables are tender.

Pour in the hot stock, then return to the oven and continue to roast for 10 minutes. Remove from the oven.

Blend all the ingredients together until smooth, adding a little more hot stock if the consistency is too thick, and check for seasoning.

Divide among four bowls and serve immediately with a final drizzle of oil.

Sunshine-Colored Vegetables 147

TORTA DI CAROTE E MANDORLE
Carrot and almond cake

Delicately light and healthy, this easy carrot cake would be perfect with a morning coffee or at teatime. I like to use the Italian raising agent known as *Paneangeli*, with its delicate vanilla flavor, and it should be obtainable from Italian delis and international grocery stores. Otherwise, regular baking powder will work just fine.

SERVES 8

4 eggs, separated
generous 1 cup (225 g) white sugar
1 cup (125 g) all-purpose flour, sifted
2 tsp Paneangeli baking powder, sifted (or regular baking powder)
1¾ cups (150 g) ground almonds
9¾ oz (275 g) carrots, grated
a little confectioners' sugar, sifted
handful of sliced almonds

Preheat the oven to 350°F (180°C). Grease an 8 in (20 cm) round springform cake pan and line it with parchment paper.

In a large bowl, whisk the egg yolks and sugar together for about 10 minutes, until nice and creamy.

In a separate bowl, whisk the egg whites until stiff.

Fold the flour, *Paneangeli* (or baking powder), ground almonds, and grated carrots into the egg yolk mixture, then fold in the stiffened egg whites.

Pour the mixture into the lined cake pan and bake in the oven for 55–60 minutes, until risen and cooked through. If you insert a wooden skewer, it should come out clean.

Remove from the oven, then leave to cool completely before carefully removing it from the pan. Place on a plate and dust the top with confectioners' sugar and a handful of sliced almonds, before serving.

TIP
This cake is best eaten fresh but will keep in an airtight container at room temperature for up to 3 days.

SFORMATINI DI CAROTE CON SALSINA VERDE
Carrot soufflés with parsley sauce

These wonderfully light and delicate carrot *sformatini* are a delight and don't sink once you take them out of the oven. In fact, you could make them in advance and simply heat them up before serving. Served with a simple parsley sauce, they make a great dinner party appetizer or a deliciously light main meal.

MAKES 8

2 lb 4 oz (1 kg) carrots, peeled and sliced into thin rounds
¼ cup (60 ml) heavy cream
5½ tbsp (80 g) butter, plus extra for greasing
6 tbsp grated Parmesan
⅔ cup (80 g) self-rising flour, sifted
2 eggs, separated
dried breadcrumbs, for dusting
sea salt and freshly ground black pepper

For the parsley sauce
1 tbsp white wine vinegar
¼ cup (60 ml) hot tap water
2½ oz (70 g) crustless stale bread
2 big handfuls of finely chopped flat-leaf parsley
¼ cup (60 ml) extra virgin olive oil
sea salt

Preheat the oven to 350°F (180°C).

Bring a pot of salted water to a boil and cook the carrot slices for about 10 minutes until tender. Drain well and blend with the heavy cream.

Melt the butter in a pot over medium-low heat, add the carrot cream and cook for a couple of minutes, stirring all the time, until the mixture begins to thicken slightly. Remove from the heat, season with salt and pepper, and stir in the cheese, flour, and egg yolks.

In a bowl, whisk the egg whites until stiff, then gently fold into the carrot mix.

Grease eight ramekins with butter and dust with breadcrumbs, then divide the soufflé mixture among them. Place the ramekins in a roasting pan, then pour water inside the pan until it reaches about halfway up the sides of the ramekins.

Bake in the oven for 35 minutes, until the soufflés have risen nicely.

Meanwhile, make the parsley sauce. In a bowl, combine the vinegar and water and soak the bread in this. Squeeze out the excess liquid, then transfer the bread to a blender with the parsley, olive oil, and a little salt and blend to make a smooth, thick sauce.

Remove the *sformatini* from the oven and carefully tip them out onto plates, then serve hot with the parsley sauce.

CAULIFLOWER
CAVOLFIORE

Just like broccoli and cabbage, cauliflower belongs to the brassica family. In fact, the Italian word is made up of *cavolo,* meaning cabbage, and *fiore* meaning flower, hence cabbage flower. It's head is made up of tiny, tightly packed flower buds, known as curd, with green leaves wrapped around the base. The curd is usually white in color, but there are green, orange, and purple varieties, too.

As a species, cauliflower is thought to originate in the Middle East in countries bordering the Mediterranean sea and became very associated with Cyprus in the Middle Ages, eventually spreading throughout Europe. Italy is a large producer and cauliflower is grown all over the country but especially in central and southern regions. Sicily produces a purple variety known as *Violetto di Sicilia,* which is a hybrid of white cauliflower and broccoli. It's especially high in antioxidants and used like white cauliflower.

Typically a winter vegetable, cauliflower has a long growing season in Italy, from around October to the end of May. It is very versatile and makes a good low-carb substitute to potatoes, plus it's a great source of vitamins and fiber. Cauliflower absorbs flavors well and, in Italy, it is used in many pasta dishes, especially in Sicily, where *Pasta ch'i Vruocculi Arriminati* is a classic dish: cauliflower is mixed with anchovies, raisins, and pine nuts and used to dress bucatini or spaghetti, then topped with breadcrumbs.

Cauliflower is delicious mashed and made into fritters or *polpette* (see page 154), roasted with spices, blended into a creamy soup, chopped and added to minestrone and cheesy bakes (see page 157), or sliced into thick chunks and seared like a steak. In Naples, cauliflower is integral to a traditional Christmas dish, *Insalata di Rinforzo*. Lightly boiled florets are combined with preserved summer vegetables, anchovies, and olives.

It is also very common to preserve cauliflower florets in vinegar and oil. They are often added to the Italian mixed vegetable pickle known as *Giardiniera,* perfect with cured meats and cheese.

Finely grated cauliflower "rice" is a popular alternative to rice or couscous. Widely available in supermarkets, it is also easy to make at home. Place the cauliflower in a food processor or grate to make "rice" grains. Use them raw or gently heat them through in a pan—this is often served as a side dish with stews or curries. The green leaves and thick stems are edible, too, and can be added to soups and stews and cooked in bakes.

How to use cauliflower:

Buying and storing
Look for firm, creamy white, unblemished heads with compact florets and crisp fresh leaves. Avoid any that are going yellow or are bruised. The size of the head makes no difference to the quality. Store in the fridge for a couple of days.

Preparing
Cooking florets takes no time at all, simply boil them for 5–8 minutes. To roast the florets, drizzle with olive oil, season with salt and pepper and any other spices, and cook for 15–20 minutes until tender. Roasting a whole cauliflower will take up to 1 hour.

GATTO' DI CAVOLFIORE
Mashed *Cauliflower* bake

This traditional Neapolitan dish is usually only made with potatoes, but the addition of cauliflower gives it a really tasty twist. You could make it with just cauliflower, but I like to keep the potato for the starchy element, or you could replace the potato with ½ cup (50 g) of dried breadcrumbs. Serve with some steamed greens or a salad on the side.

SERVES 4

3 tbsp butter, plus extra for greasing
1 tbsp dried breadcrumbs, plus extra for dusting
1 medium-sized cauliflower (or 1 lb 2 oz/500 g florets)
1 lb 2 oz (500 g) potatoes, peeled and cut into chunks
⅓ cup (80 ml) hot milk
¼ cup (30 g) grated Parmesan
pinch of grated nutmeg
2 tsp finely chopped flat-leaf parsley
1 x 4½ oz (125 g) ball of mozzarella cheese, drained—½ sliced, ½ roughly chopped
4 slices of cooked ham (approx. 5½ oz/150 g)—2 slices roughly chopped, 2 slices left whole
sea salt and freshly ground black pepper

Preheat the oven to 400°F (200°C). Lightly grease a baking dish (approx. 8 in x 8 in/20 cm x 20 cm) with some butter and dust with breadcrumbs.

If you are using a whole cauliflower, break into florets. Bring a pot of salted water to a boil and cook the florets and potatoes until tender, then drain and steam-dry for a couple of minutes to ensure all the excess water is removed.

Mash the potato and cauliflower together while still hot, then mix in the hot milk, butter, Parmesan, nutmeg, parsley, chopped mozzarella, and chopped ham and season with salt and pepper to taste.

Place half of the mixture in the prepared baking dish and layer with the remaining ham and mozzarella slices, then top with the remaining mixture. Sprinkle with the breadcrumbs and bake in the oven for 45 minutes, until a golden crust forms on top. Serve hot.

TIP
This is the perfect dish for using up leftovers—add whatever cured meats or cheese you have in the fridge.

POLPETTE DI CAVOLFIORE
Cauliflower "polpette"

These cauliflower "meatballs" or *polpette* are so delicious that I'm sure they will appeal to both young and old and you'll need to make more! The paprika gives a little kick to the cauliflower but you could use herbs or other flavorings, if you prefer. They're very simple to make and are a great way of using up any leftover cooked cauliflower. Serve with a mixed salad and rustic bread.

MAKES 15

1 small cauliflower, broken into florets
1 medium-sized potato, peeled and cut into small chunks
3 eggs
¼ cup (30 g) grated Parmesan
1 tsp paprika (optional)
abundant dried breadcrumbs
all-purpose flour, for dusting
abundant sunflower or vegetable oil, for frying
sea salt and freshly ground black pepper

Bring a pot of salted water to a boil and cook the cauliflower florets and potato until tender, then drain well (if necessary, pat the cauliflower dry with a clean kitchen towel).

Mash the cauliflower and potato together with 1 egg, the Parmesan, paprika, and ½ tablespoon of breadcrumbs and season with salt and pepper. With your hands, form the mixture into small balls (*polpette*), each roughly the size of a walnut.

Lightly beat the remaining eggs with a little salt. First dust the *polpette* in flour, then dip in the egg and finally roll in the breadcrumbs to coat.

Sprinkle some breadcrumbs to cover the base of a flat plate or tray, arrange the *polpette* on top, and chill in the fridge for at least 30 minutes.

Heat plenty of oil in a deep frying pan over medium-high heat until hot, then deep-fry the *polpette* in batches for about 5 minutes until golden. Drain on paper towels and serve.

CAVOLFIORE AL FORNO CON FUNGHI E FORMAGGIO

Italian *cauliflower* cheese with mushrooms

I love cauliflower cheese with a Sunday roast dinner. It was a completely novel dish to me when I first came to England, but I've loved it since. This is my Italian version, with the addition of sautéed mushrooms, Parmesan, and mozzarella.

SERVES 4

1 medium-sized cauliflower (or 1 lb 2 oz/500 g cauliflower florets)
3 tbsp extra virgin olive oil
2 garlic cloves, finely diced
9 oz (250 g) cremini mushrooms, finely sliced
handful of flat-leaf parsley, finely chopped
1 x 4½ oz (125 g) ball of mozzarella cheese, drained and roughly chopped
sea salt

For the béchamel
3 tbsp butter
⅓ cup (40 g) all-purpose flour
2 cups (500 ml) milk
½ cup (50 g) grated Parmesan
sea salt and freshly ground black pepper

Preheat the oven to 400°F (200°C).

Break up the cauliflower head into florets and set aside.

Heat the olive oil in a frying pan over medium heat and sweat the garlic, then add the mushrooms and a little salt and stir-fry for 5 minutes. Remove from the heat and stir in the parsley.

Make the béchamel. In a saucepan, melt the butter over low heat, then remove and whisk in the flour to make a smooth paste. Gradually add the milk, then return to the heat, whisking, until the sauce thickens. Remove from the heat, season, and stir in all but 2 tablespoons of the Parmesan.

Mix the mushrooms, cauliflower, three-quarters of the béchamel, and the mozzarella. Place in a baking dish. Pour over the remaining béchamel; sprinkle with the remaining Parmesan. Cover with foil and bake for 50 minutes.

Increase the oven temperature to 425°F (220°C), remove the foil, and bake for 15 minutes, until golden.

Leave to rest for 5 minutes and serve.

TIP Don't boil the cauliflower first. There's no need and can make the final result quite watery—let the oven do its job!

MUSHROOMS
FUNGHI

When Italians talk about mushrooms, they usually refer to the wild variety, of which there are many different types. Wild mushrooms grow all over Italy but especially in Piemonte, Lombardy, Veneto, Emilia Romagna, Liguria, and Tuscany, as well as in the south in the Calabrian Sila forests. Wild mushrooms are taken very seriously in Italy, so much so that, in the forest area between Emilia Romagna and Tuscany, the highly prized *Borgotaro* porcino mushroom has been given protected IGP status.

Italians love to forage for wild mushrooms and, during the season, it is not uncommon for people to head to the forests, armed with their baskets in search of "meaty" porcini (ceps or penny bun), pretty yellow chanterelles, large parasol mushrooms, magical puffballs, and clusters of honey fungus.

The UK is also blessed with a multitude of wild mushrooms and I love nothing more than venturing out on a glorious fall morning to see what I can find. If you forage your area, be very careful and NEVER pick wild mushrooms unless you know exactly what you are picking; not all wild mushrooms are edible. Unfortunately, in Italy, a few people die of poisoning every year. Unless you are knowledgeable or have an expert on fungi with you who can advise, I would simply enjoy the forest walks and then visit a specialist grocery store or market to buy them, even though they can be expensive.

When I don't go foraging, I am also very happy with the cultivated mushrooms that are available all year round. White button, chestnut or cremini, and large Portobello mushrooms are inexpensive and abundant in shops everywhere, and these are the types I have used in the recipes in this book. Some larger supermarkets also stock cultivated oyster and shiitake mushrooms.

Italy is well known for truffles (white and black), which are also fungi that grow underground, and for which we need the help of specialist dogs to sniff out from the earth. The central regions of Tuscany, Umbria, and the Marche are famous for the black truffle, and the northern Piemonte region is home to the very expensive white Alba truffle. Italians love truffle delicately shaved over pasta and risotto or cooked with eggs. It's quite tricky to describe the taste; the white is stronger than the black, but both are earthy and nutty with a musky scent. You either love them or hate them, but you should try them at least once in your life, if you can.

Mushrooms are a strange, mysterious species. No one really knows their origins but they have probably been around since earth began and they have a habit of appearing in the same place each year. Although we treat mushrooms as vegetables, they really are not—they don't come from plants and they "steal" their nutrients from living and dead matter on the forest floor, such as decaying leaves and tree trunks. The Ancient Romans adored them, especially Julius Caesar, and a particular bright orange type, now known as *Amanita Caesarea,* was named in his honor.

It was not until around the eighteenth century that the common field (white button) mushroom began to be cultivated in France and quite by chance, apparently. However, thereafter it spread to Italy and the rest of Europe. Dark, damp, and humid environments are ideal for a lot of mushrooms and so, in these early days, caves provided excellent growing conditions. Over time, mushroom farms rapidly expanded and cultivated mushrooms are now usually grown indoors, in order to provide a constant supply to supermarkets all year round.

Whether you opt for the wild or cultivated variety, mushrooms are a good source of nutrients and ideal for all plant-based diets as their texture makes a great meat substitute. A mushroom ragù is often served with fresh, steaming, gooey polenta or added to lasagne in place of meat (see page 163). Italians, in fact, love to add mushrooms to many dishes, and especially a little dried porcini to bring that umami "forest" flavor. Mushrooms can be filled and baked (see page 165) or dipped in egg and breadcrumbs and deep-fried as a treat. They are lovely in frittatas, savory pies, stir-fries and stews, or blended into a creamy soup. They go with most flavors and combine well with meat, fish, and legumes. A simple way to cook them is to sauté them in oil, garlic, and parsley, which is often known as *trifolati* in Italy. Cultivated mushrooms can also be thinly sliced and eaten raw in a salad, simply dressed with extra virgin olive oil, and lemon juice.

How to use mushrooms:

Buying and storing
When buying mushrooms, make sure they are firm and fresh looking. Also, give them a sniff if you can; they should smell fresh and earthy. Try to use them on the day of purchase or store them in the fridge for 3–4 days. Never wash mushrooms; only use a damp cloth to remove the dirt.

Preparing
If you've picked your own wild mushrooms, it is best to cook them on the same day if you can. Again, don't wash them, use a damp cloth to remove the dirt and cut out any parts that have decayed. If you've picked lots, then preserve them. I like to pickle them, but first they need to be boiled before combining with garlic, chile, and oil and placed in sterilized jars. These make a lovely antipasto that you can enjoy all year round.

ARANCINI DI FUNGHI
Filled *mushroom* balls

These filled mushrooms may seem a little fussy to make but, believe me, they are well worth the effort! Once filled, the mushrooms are pressed together to form a ball or, as I've called them in Italian, *arancini* (little oranges). I like to serve them with a selection of salads and pickles. You can easily make these vegetarian by omitting the pork and Parmesan, and substituting extra breadcrumbs and chopped mushrooms.

MAKES 8

16 small-medium chestnut or white mushrooms (approx. 1 lb 2 oz/ 500 g), wiped clean
2 tbsp extra virgin olive oil
pat of butter
3½ oz (100 g) ground pork
2 sage leaves, finely chopped
4 tsp white wine
¼ cup (50 g) ricotta
¼ cup (30 g) grated Parmesan
all-purpose flour, for dusting
3 eggs, lightly beaten
abundant dried breadcrumbs, enough to coat the mushrooms
abundant vegetable oil, for frying
sea salt and freshly ground black pepper

Remove the stalks from the mushrooms and, using a small spoon, very carefully remove as much of the interior (gills) as possible without tearing the mushrooms. Finely chop the stalks and combine with the gills.

Heat the olive oil and butter in a small frying pan, add the chopped mushroom stems and gills, and stir-fry for a couple of minutes over medium heat until softened. Remove from the pan and set aside.

Replace the frying pan on the heat, add the ground pork and sage, and stir-fry until the meat is well seared. Season with salt and pepper, then add the wine, stir, and allow to evaporate. Add the cooked mushrooms to the pan and cook for a minute, then take off the heat, allow to cool, and stir in the ricotta and Parmesan.

Fill the mushrooms with this mixture. Join two mushrooms together, pressing well, then coat in flour, dip in beaten egg, and repeat to double-coat. Finally, coat in breadcrumbs.

Heat plenty of vegetable oil in a deep, heavy-based pan over medium-high heat until hot, then deep-fry the mushroom balls for about 4 minutes until golden brown. A deep-fryer is ideal for this if you have one!

Using a slotted spoon, lift the mushroom balls out of the oil, drain well on paper towels to soak up the excess oil, and then serve immediately.

PASTICCIO DI POLENTA E FUNGHI
Polenta lasagne with *mushrooms*

The Italian title of this dish—*pasticcio*—means a "mess" because, when serving, it really can look messy on the plate! However, it is delicious and the perfect winter warmer, so don't let this deter you! The layering is similar to a lasagne but the pasta sheets are swapped for polenta, which makes it ideal for anyone on a gluten-free diet. It can easily be made in advance and reheated, and this often makes it easier to serve (not so messy!).

SERVES 6–8

3⅓ cups (800 ml) water
7 oz (200 g) instant polenta cornmeal
2 tbsp butter, plus extra for greasing
1 x 4½ oz (125 g) ball of mozzarella cheese, drained and roughly chopped
2 oz (60 g) Parmesan, grated, plus extra to garnish
pinch of sea salt
fresh herbs, to garnish (optional)

For the mushroom ragù
3 tbsp extra virgin olive oil
½ onion, finely chopped
1 oz (30 g) pancetta, finely chopped
leaves of 1 thyme sprig
1 lb 2 oz (500 g) chestnut mushrooms, sliced
3 cups (700 ml) tomato passata
sea salt and freshly ground black pepper

For this recipe, you will need a deep, rectangular baking dish (approx. 7 in x 9½ in/18 cm x 24 cm), as well as three shallow trays or dishes that are the same size (but they don't have to be as deep)—these will be molds for the thin polenta layers. Lightly grease your three rectangular-shaped trays or dishes and set aside for use later on.

First make the mushroom ragù. Heat the olive oil in a heavy-based pot and sweat the onion, pancetta, and thyme over medium heat for a couple of minutes, until the pancetta begins to color. Stir in the mushrooms, season with salt and pepper, and then stir-fry over medium-high heat for 2–3 minutes. Add the tomato passata with a little water (rinsed out of the jar), then cover with a lid and cook over gentle heat for 1 hour.

Continued overleaf

Meanwhile, preheat the oven to 400°F (200°C) and prepare the polenta. Place the water in a pot, add the salt, and bring to a boil, then gradually whisk in the polenta and cook for a couple of minutes until thickened—check the instructions on the package. Remove from the heat before mixing in the butter.

Divide the polenta mixture among the three prepared dishes, then level out and smooth the top with an oiled spatula. Leave to cool for 30 minutes or so.

Lightly grease the baking dish with oil and line with one of the polenta layers. Top with a third of the mushroom ragù, followed by some mozzarella and Parmesan. Continue making layers like these until you have used up all the ingredients, finishing with a layer of cheese on top.

Bake in the oven for 30 minutes, until the top is nicely golden and bubbling, then remove from the oven and leave to rest for 10 minutes. Garnish with some extra grated Parmesan and fresh chopped herbs before serving.

TIP
I use chestnut mushrooms, but you can use whatever variety you like, or a mixture.

164 Sunshine-Colored Vegetables

FUNGHI RIPIENI AL FORNO
Filled baked *mushrooms*

Filled Portobello mushrooms make a wonderful, nourishing main course, and the combination of smoky scamorza and spicy salami brings a pleasant flavor kick. I use a spicy salami from Calabria, but you could use chorizo or any other spicy cured sausage. Of course, if you prefer, you can omit the salami and just fill with more onion, bread, and cheese.

SERVES 4

8 large Portobello-type mushrooms
1 tbsp extra virgin olive oil, plus extra for greasing and drizzling
½ onion, finely chopped
leaves of 2 thyme sprigs
2 oz (60 g) spicy Calabrian-type salami, finely chopped
3 oz (80 g) scamorza cheese, cut into small cubes
¼ cup (30 g) grated Parmesan
3 oz (80 g) stale bread, soaked in a little warm water to soften

For the topping
1½ tbsp dried breadcrumbs
1½ tbsp grated Parmesan
leaves of 2 whole small thyme sprigs

Preheat the oven to 400°F (200°C). Lightly grease a large enough baking dish or a couple of baking pans with a little olive oil

Remove the stalks from the mushrooms and, using a small spoon, very carefully remove as much of the interior (gills) as possible without tearing the mushrooms. Finely chop the stalks and combine with the gills.

Heat the olive oil in a small frying pan over medium heat and sweat the onion for 2 minutes, then add the finely chopped mushrooms and thyme leaves and stir-fry for a further couple of minutes, until cooked.

Remove from the heat and combine with the salami, scamorza, Parmesan, and softened bread.

Lightly grease the inside of the mushrooms. Stuff the mushrooms with the filling and then place in the prepared baking dish.

Combine the topping ingredients and sprinkle over each mushroom, then drizzle with a little olive oil, cover with foil, and bake for 25 minutes, until the mushrooms are cooked through.

Remove the foil and place under a hot broiler for about 5 minutes until nicely golden. Serve immediately.

ONIONS
CIPOLLE

The humble onion is probably the vegetable that we pay least attention to, yet we use it so much! It flavors a myriad of dishes and forms the basis of so many sauces, soups, and stews that it truly doesn't get the credit it deserves. However, it does take center stage in many Italian dishes and, in the Neapolitan classic *La Genovese* (see page 168), a couple of kilos of onions are slow-cooked and broken down into a deliciously thick pasta sauce.

Onions are believed to originate in Asia and, as part of the Allium family, are one of the world's oldest cultivated plants. The Romans introduced them to Europe and regarded them highly, both as a food and a medicine; they were also used to treat a variety of ailments. Even today, the liquid from boiling onions is used as a natural cold remedy.

In Italy, onions were traditionally viewed as food of the poor and a saying emerged, *pane e cipolla,* which translates as "bread and onion" and meant, if you had these two ingredients, you could survive.

Today, many different varieties of onion are grown throughout Italy. The *Cipolla di Tropea,* from the Calabrian seaside town of the same name, is a red variety, oval in shape and with a wonderfully sweet and mild taste—I love to eat it raw. Sicily grows huge white onions, each weighing over 1 lb 2 oz (500 g), called *Cipolla di Giarratana*. They also have a sweet taste and are used to fill *scacce*, a traditional Sicilian flat focaccia-type bread. They are also excellent baked. The *Cipolla Dorata di Parma* have a golden color and are mostly used as a base for sauces. The *Cipolle Borettane,* from Reggio Emilia, are small and flat and commonly preserved or used in *agrodolce* dishes (sweet and sour). I could go on, but essentially, golden-skinned onions tend to taste strongest and are best suited for sauce bases and slow-cooking, whereas white and red onions are milder and sweeter in taste and more suited to eating raw.

Cipolotti are also common in Italy. They are similar to a scallion but the bulb is often thicker and, in Italian cooking, they are often braised with other vegetables, or roasted or added to stews. *Scalogni* (shallots) are also used in dishes that require a sweeter taste; either banana shallots or the smaller round ones.

Onions are so versatile in Italian cooking. They can be stuffed and baked, blended into soup, added to savory pies (see page 170) and tarts, used to top focaccia and pizza, as well as incorporated into a multitude of pasta dishes. Risotto always begins with a little chopped onion as its base, regardless of what other ingredients might be used, and *Pasta e fagioli* is sometimes topped with a little raw onion to provide a crunchy contrast to the soft pasta and beans. Whole onions are always added to *bollito* (boiled meats) and then enjoyed with other vegetables, drizzled with a little extra virgin olive oil. I like to marinade finely sliced onions in red wine vinegar for about an hour, then add them to a warm potato salad. The onions soften and take on a lovely tangy flavor. You can leave them to marinate for longer, stored in a sealed container in the fridge, where they will last at least a week or so. They are delicious added to salads and grilled cheese sandwiches.

How to use onions:

Buying and storing

When buying, choose firm onions with dry, papery skins. Avoid any that are soft or display blemishes, or ones that are sprouting. Once home, store in a dry, cool, well-ventilated place, if you can. A cellar, garage, or shed is ideal, especially if you have lots to store—they can last for a couple of months if stored correctly. Avoid putting them in the fridge as they tend to deteriorate quickly. The only time to put them in the fridge is if you have leftover cut onions—in which case, wrap tightly in plastic or place in an airtight container and use within a couple of days.

Preparing

As a rule, the longer you cook onions for, the sweeter they become as they slowly release their sugars. If frying, keep the heat gentle and take care not to let them burn; burned onions are bitter tasting and will ruin your final dish. Onions exude their own liquid so keep the temperature low and, if your recipe requires the onions to cook for a long time, cover with a lid. Then be patient; they will steam-fry by themselves.

LA GENOVESE "SCAPPATA" CON ZITI
Ziti pasta with *onions*

This is a vegetarian version of the traditional slow-cooked *Genovese* meat sauce. Despite its name, the recipe comes from Naples and, apparently, was made by the Neapolitans for sailors coming from Genova in the days of the maritime republics. It was probably made with inferior cuts of meat and, to mask the flavor, lots of onions. These days, *Genovese* sauce is made with veal, pork, or beef, but I also like it meat-free. The magic of slow cooking transforms the onions into a deliciously sweet, thick, rich sauce, which is perfect for dressing pasta.

SERVES 4–6

scant ½ cup (100 ml) extra virgin olive oil
4 fresh or dried bay leaves
4 lb 8 oz (2 kg) brown or white onions, thinly sliced
14 oz (400 g) ziti pasta, broken up
sea salt and freshly ground black pepper
grated pecorino cheese (or a vegetarian pecorino-style cheese), to serve

Heat the olive oil with the bay leaves in a large pot over medium heat and stir in the onions. Reduce the heat, cover with a lid, and leave to cook gently for 2½ hours. Stir from time to time, and season with salt and pepper.

If, at the end of the cooking time, you find that there is still quite a bit of liquid left, remove the lid and cook over medium heat for about 20 minutes until the excess liquid has evaporated. Discard the bay leaves.

Meanwhile, bring a pot of salted water to a boil and cook the *ziti* until al dente. Drain and add the pasta to the onion sauce, mixing well over the heat for a minute or so to combine.

Serve with a sprinkling of grated pecorino and black pepper.

TIP
The traditional pasta used for this sauce is the long tubular shapes, known as *ziti* or *candele,* which are then broken up. However, you can use penne if these are difficult to find.

TORTA SALATA DI CIPOLLE
Onion pie

It's amazing what you can do with onions and a few basic extra ingredients. The idea of this onion pie is based on a traditional dish from Puglia commonly known as *Calzone di Cipolle* using onions as the main ingredient, *ricotta forte*, a strong local cheese, and whatever other ingredients you have on hand. My version includes strong provolone cheese, olives, and hard-boiled egg. If you can't get provolone, use any hard cheese you have available. Serve with a green salad for a nutritious meal.

SERVES 8

1½ tbsp butter, plus extra for greasing
1 tbsp extra virgin olive oil
1 lb 9 oz (700 g) onions, finely sliced
leaves of 3 thyme sprigs
1½ tbsp dried breadcrumbs, plus extra for dusting
3 tbsp (20 g) grated Parmesan
2 eggs, lightly beaten
10½ oz (300 g) ready-made shortcrust pastry, thawed if frozen
all-purpose flour, for dusting
¾ oz (20 g) pitted black olives
1 cold hard-boiled egg, peeled and thinly sliced
1¾ oz (50 g) provolone picante cheese, finely sliced
ground black pepper

Preheat the oven to 375°F (190°C). Lightly butter a round pie dish or pan (approx. 8 in/20 cm in diameter) and dust with breadcrumbs.

Heat the butter and oil in a large frying pan over medium heat and stir-fry the onions for a couple of minutes. Reduce the heat to low, cover with a lid, and cook for 20–25 minutes, until the onions have completely softened. Remove from the heat and leave to cool. Add the thyme leaves, breadcrumbs, Parmesan, and beaten eggs, season with pepper, and mix well together.

Roll out the pastry on a lightly floured work surface to a ¼ in (5 mm) thickness, then line the prepared pie dish with the pastry. Trim off the excess, then collect in a ball and roll out again to create a pie lid. Set aside.

Fill the pastry base with half the onion filling, scatter over the olives, and top with the hard-boiled egg and half the provolone slices. Top the remaining onion filling, then the remaining provolone. Cover with the pastry and crimp the edges to seal.

Bake in the oven for 40 minutes, until golden. When cooked, leave to rest for about 5 minutes, then slice and serve.

POTATOES
PATATE

Potatoes originated in Peru thousands of years ago and were introduced to Europe by the Spanish in the 1500s. However, people were suspicious of this tuber from the nightshade family, using it mainly as a plant in botanical gardens or for livestock fodder. It wasn't until the 1800s that potatoes were used in Italian kitchens.

Potatoes are grown throughout Italy but especially in the northern alpine regions, and some of the best are grown in the fertile soils of the mountainous Sila area of Calabria. There are many varieties. Italians favor white or yellow-skinned potatoes, but purple ones are grown, too, and the *Blu di Valtellina*, an ancient variety from the Alps, is making a comeback for its many health benefits. The Puglian province of Lecce produces the notable *Patata Novella di Galatina:* a potato low in starch with a delicate flavor.

Sweet potatoes are used in much the same way as potatoes. They originated in the Americas and are grown in Italy in Veneto and Puglia and known as *patata dolce* or *patata Americana*. Gnocchi can be made with sweet potato, and it is often blended into soups, added to pasta dishes, or enjoyed baked or roasted with garlic and chile. Its sweetness makes it good in desserts and cakes, too (see page 174).

Potatoes come in two main varieties, starchy and waxy. Starchy potatoes are best used for roasting, baking, making fries, or mashing. In Italy, popular varieties are *Tonda di Napoli* or *Comasca Bianca*, which are similar to Russets or Idaho potatoes. Red-skinned potatoes are a good all-rounder. Waxy potatoes contain less starch so are ideal for boiling or malking potato salads and layered bakes.

Potatoes might not spring to mind when thinking about Italian cuisine, but they do play a significant part in Italian cooking. Think gnocchi—served with melted butter, pesto, or a tomato sauce. Italians also love potato bakes like the Neapolitan *Gatto' di Patate*, a mashed potato cake combined with cheese, cured meats, eggs, and black pepper. In Puglia, *Tiella* is a potato bake with onions, tomatoes, mussels, and rice.

Italians love to roast potatoes with olive oil, garlic, and rosemary, or cook them in a pan on the stovetop. I like to coat potato cubes in semolina and grated Parmesan before roasting. In Puglia, mashed potatoes are sometimes added to focaccia for a softer dough, and sliced potatoes are sometimes added to the topping (see page 178).

How to use potatoes:

Buying and storing
Avoid potatoes that appear green and are soft or sprouting. Once home, store in a cool, dark, dry, well-ventilated place—a cellar or outside shed or garage is ideal. Store them in a paper bag, bowl, or basket to allow air to circulate and stop early decay. Stored correctly, potatoes can last a couple of months or more. Don't store them in the fridge as the chill turns the starch into sugar.

Preparing
Italians tend to boil the whole potato with the skin on, which is peeled off once the potato is cooled. You don't need to peel potatoes, just wash them; the skin is edible and nutritious. Try roasting potato peelings with a little olive oil and salt for a crispy snack.

PATATE NAPOLETANE AL FORNO
Potato bake with tomatoes and capers

This simple potato bake makes an ideal accompaniment to roast meats but can also be eaten on its own with a crunchy green salad or some steamed green beans.

SERVES 2–4

14 oz (400 g) potatoes, any kind, thinly sliced into approx. ⅛ in (3 mm) thick rounds
1 small red onion, finely sliced
scant ½ cup (100 ml) tomato passata
2 tsp capers
2 tbsp extra virgin olive oil, plus extra for greasing and drizzling
1 garlic clove, finely diced
1 tsp dried oregano
sea salt and freshly ground black pepper

Preheat the oven to 400°F (200°C).

Place the sliced potatoes in a large bowl with the rest of the ingredients and gently mix together with your hands.

Lightly grease a baking dish (approx. 7 in x 8½ in/18 cm x 22 cm) with a little olive oil, then add the potato mixture, spreading it out evenly, and drizzle a little extra oil over the top. Cover with foil and bake in the oven for 40 minutes, then remove the foil and continue to bake for a further 5–10 minutes, until golden.

Remove from the oven, leave to rest for 5 minutes, then serve.

TORTA DI PATATA DOLCE E CIOCCOLATO

Sweet *potato* and chocolate loaf cake

Sweet potato was not an ingredient I was familiar with when growing up in Italy. However, now its popularity is growing, I love it in both savory and sweet dishes. Combined with dark chocolate and lemon zest, this simple teatime loaf cake is a delight and can also be enjoyed with an espresso for breakfast.

SERVES 6–8

- 1 large sweet potato (total weight approx. 10½ oz/300 g)
- 3 eggs
- ¾ cup (150 g) white sugar
- zest of 1 lemon
- 10 tbsp (150 g) butter, melted
- 2 cups (225 g) "00" flour, sifted
- 1 x ½ oz (16 g) envelope Paneangeli baking powder, sifted, or use 4 tsp regular baking powder
- 2 oz (60 g) dark chocolate, finely chopped

Preheat the oven to 350°F (180°C) and line a 9 in x 5½ in (900 g) loaf pan with parchment paper.

First, cook the sweet potato. Either bake it in the oven for 50 minutes or so, whole in its skin, or boil it in a pot of water for about 40 minutes until tender. Alternatively, for speed, peel it, chop into small chunks, and place in a bowl with about a tablespoon of water, then microwave it for about 8 minutes until tender. When cooked, mash the potato, then set aside.

Place the eggs and sugar in a bowl and beat until creamy and fluffy. Gradually whisk in the mashed sweet potato, the lemon zest, and melted butter until well incorporated, then fold in the flour, baking powder, and chocolate.

Pour the mixture into the prepared pan and bake in the oven for about 50 minutes, until well risen and golden on top. Insert a wooden skewer; if it comes out clean, the cake is ready.

Leave to cool in the pan, then carefully remove, slice, and serve.

PANZAROTTI NAPOLETANI

Neopolitan *potato* croquettes

These Neapolitan potato croquettes are such a delicious treat! Really simple to prepare with pantry ingredients, you can serve them as a side dish or enjoy them with a fresh crunchy mixed salad of your choice. You may not need the whole mozzarella ball, and make sure it's well drained and patted dry with paper towels or a clean kitchen towel before using.

MAKES 8

1 lb 2 oz (500 g) potatoes suitable for mashing
1 tbsp finely chopped flat-leaf parsley, plus extra to garnish
2½ tbsp grated pecorino cheese or Parmesan
1 egg yolk, plus 2 egg whites
1 x 4½ oz (125 g) ball of mozzarella cheese, drained, patted dry and sliced lengthways into 8 thin strips
all-purpose flour, for dusting
abundant dried breadcrumbs, for coating
abundant vegetable oil, for deep-frying
sea salt and freshly ground black pepper

Bring a large pot of salted water to a boil and cook the potatoes in their skins until tender. Drain well, cool slightly, and remove the skins, then return to the pot, season with salt and pepper, and mash. Add the parsley, hard cheese, and egg yolk and, with your hands, knead well like you would a dough.

Take a piece of the potato dough, approx. 2 oz (55 g) in weight and shape each into a fat sausage. With the help of your index or middle finger, make an indent lengthways down into the middle and insert a strip of mozzarella, then roll with your hands to cover the mozzarella with the potato dough. Repeat this process until you have used up all the mixture.

Lightly beat the egg whites in a bowl. Dust each croquette first in flour, then dip into the beaten egg whites, and finally roll in breadcrumbs to coat. When they are all coated, place the croquettes in the fridge for at least 10 minutes to rest and harden slightly.

Heat plenty of vegetable oil in a deep, heavy-based pot until hot, then deep-fry the *panzarotti* for 3–4 minutes until golden all over. Drain well on paper towels to soak up the excess oil, then garnish with parsley and serve immediately.

CROCANTELLA DI PATATE
Crispy *potato* "focaccia"

This unleavened focaccia-type bread is really simple and quick to prepare. You can enjoy it as a snack at any time or as part of an antipasto with cured meats and cheese. It can be made in advance and reheated just before serving so that it retains its delicious crispiness.

SERVES 4–8

extra virgin olive oil, for drizzling, plus extra for greasing
fine polenta cornmeal, for dusting
1 onion, finely sliced
needles of 3 small rosemary sprigs
9½ oz (270 g) potatoes, any kind, peeled and very thinly sliced
1¾ cups (220 g) "00" flour or all-purpose flour
1¼ cups (290 ml) water, at room temperature
sea salt and freshly ground black pepper

Preheat the oven to 400°F (200°C). Lightly grease a 11 in (28 cm) round cake pan with olive oil and dust with fine polenta.

Heat a drizzle of olive oil in a small frying pan over medium heat and sweat the onion and rosemary for about 5 minutes until softened. Remove from the heat, transfer to a bowl, and combine with the potato slices. Season with salt and pepper.

Place the flour in another bowl and gradually whisk in the water until you obtain a smooth, batter-type consistency. Fold in the potato mixture.

Pour the mixture into the prepared pan and level the top. Sprinkle with a little fine polenta and drizzle with a little olive oil. Bake in the oven for 50 minutes, then increase the temperature to 460°F (240°C) and continue to bake for 10 minutes, until golden and crisp.

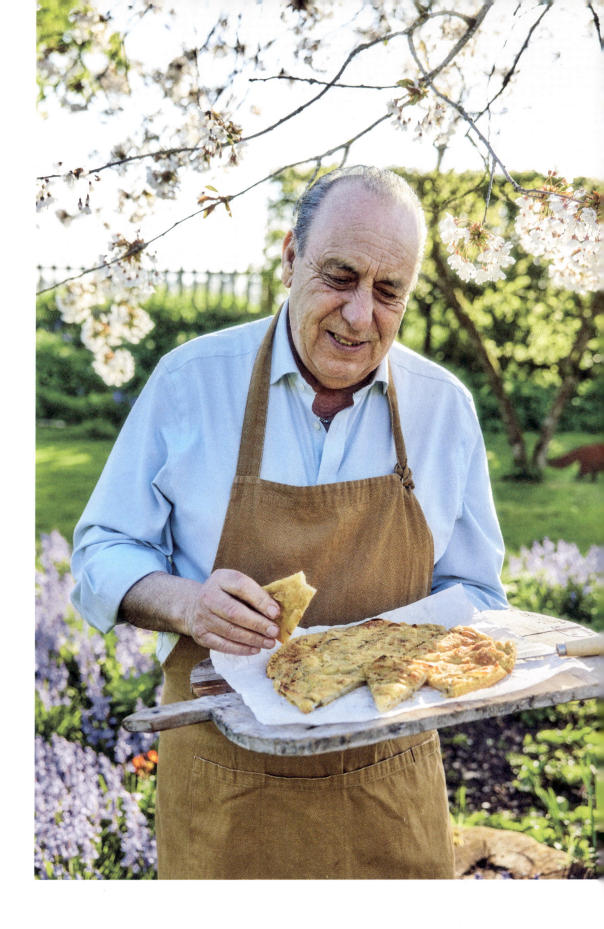

PATATE RIPIENE AL FORNO
Italian-style baked *potatoes*

Rubbing the potatoes with oil and salt before baking creates a delicious crispy skin. Be careful when scooping out the soft potato to ensure you don't break the skin. Serve with a mixed salad for a delicious meal.

SERVES 4

4 large baking potatoes
extra virgin olive oil, for rubbing and greasing
6 sun-dried tomatoes, finely chopped
2 oz (60 g) spicy salami, cooked ham, or other cured meats, finely chopped
3 oz (90 g) dolcelatte or Gorgonzola cheese
approx. 1½ tbsp grated Parmesan, for sprinkling
sea salt and freshly ground black pepper

Preheat the oven to 425°F (220°C).

Scrub the potatoes and dry well with a clean kitchen towel. Prick the potatoes with a fork, then rub with a little olive oil and salt. Bake in the hot oven for 50–60 minutes, until cooked through and the skins are crispy.

Remove the potatoes from the oven and leave to rest until they are cool enough to handle. Cut in half, lengthways, and scoop the soft potato inside into a bowl, ensuring you don't break the skin.

Mash the soft potato until smooth and combine with the sun-dried tomatoes, salami, and cheese, then season to taste. Fill the potato skins with the filling and sprinkle with the Parmesan.

Lightly grease a baking sheet with a little olive oil and arrange the filled potato skins on top. Return to the oven and bake for a further 10–15 minutes until golden, then serve immediately.

PUMPKIN/SQUASH
ZUCCA

In Italy, pumpkins are not just adornments for Halloween (although they do look lovely lit up on windowsills, bringing cheer to dark evenings). In fact, the whole trick-or-treat business is quite alien to me as, in my calendar, October 31st will always be the eve of All Saints, when I place candles outside. Still, younger generations of Italians have embraced Halloween and kids, dressed up in costumes and going from house to house, are now a common sight in towns and villages throughout Italy, as are decorated pumpkins.

Squash originated as a wild plant in Central America and were an important food staple among Native Americans. They were then brought to Europe by Christopher Columbus. Gourds, which are from the same family as squash, were popular with the Ancient Romans, who would carefully scoop out the flesh and then dry out the hard skin to use as containers. Maybe that's why we carve pumpkins now—who knows?

Squashes come in all shapes, sizes, and colors—smooth-skinned and knobbly, round, long, oval-shaped, big, small, and green, stripy, yellow, orange, and beige; the list goes on. Pumpkins are grown all over Italy. Northern areas around Cremona and Mantova produce some excellent varieties, like *Zucca Mantovana* (winter squash) and *Zucca Delica*. *Zucca di Chioggia,* with its distinct knobbly skin, comes from Venice and, further south in the Naples area, *Zucca Lunga di Napoli* is an elongated, green-skinned pumpkin with very few seeds and a deliciously sweet yellow flesh. In the south, pumpkins are known as *cocozza*, which, in the local dialect, also means "head."

Look out for the classic light grey Crown Prince or the smaller, orange-colored onion squash and green acorn squash varieties. Some specialty grocery stores stock the green, hard-skinned Italian *Delica* variety. It can be a bit tricky to peel but its bright orange flesh, once cooked, has a wonderfully soft, creamy consistency with a rich flavor. Also, the one variety you find all year round is the trusty oval-shaped, beige-colored butternut squash, with its sweet, nutty taste and thin, easy-to-peel skin.

Easy to grow, nutritious, and a good filler, pumpkins were traditionally seen as a food of the poor. However, with a little creativity, their sweet, nutty flesh combines well with so many flavors—rosemary, sage, garlic, chile, balsamic and wine vinegars, pancetta, Parmesan, tomatoes, and so much more. Therefore, Italians take pumpkin season seriously and enjoy this autumnal vegetable in all sorts of ways in their cooking.

Tortelli di Zucca (pumpkin-filled pasta parcels) is a popular dish in Lombardy and Emilia Romagna, along with pumpkin risotto and gnocchi (see page 186). Pumpkin is enjoyed in pasta dishes as well as blended in creamy soups (see page 187), enjoyed as fritters, added to savory pies and meat and vegetable stews, as well as served in warm salads (see page 190) and *agrodolce* (sweet and sour) dishes. Its sweetness is also perfect in desserts and cakes and sweet pies, like the ones that are so popular in America.

How to use pumpkins and squash:

Buying and storing

Look for firm, heavy pumpkins/squash without any blemishes on the skin. Whole pumpkins/squashes will last for months if stored in a cool, dry place. Sometimes, shops or markets sell pumpkin in portions or ready-cubed, which is perfectly fine, but you will need to use it immediately or store in the fridge, well wrapped, and use within a day or so.

Preparing

If you are roasting pumpkin or other winter squash, there is no need to remove the skin. Simply cut into quarters or smaller segments and remove the seeds, then arrange on a baking sheet with a little olive oil and seasonings. The hard skin will soften and be easy to remove once cooked. All winter squash skin is, in fact, edible, it's just a question of texture and if it appeals to you.

If you are frying pumpkin, cut into smaller pieces and remove the hard skin and seeds, then cut into cubes or segments and cook according to your recipe. Cutting pumpkin can be quite a hazardous job, so use a sharp knife, and be careful! Don't throw the seeds away as these are packed with vitamins and can easily be used. Simply boil them for about 5 minutes, then drain well, pat dry, and toss in a roasting pan with a little olive oil, salt, and other flavorings of your choice. Roast in a hot oven for about 10 minutes. They are delicious added to soups, sprinkled over salads, or simply enjoyed as a wholesome snack.

GNOCCHI DI ZUCCA
Pumpkin gnocchi

Pumpkin gnocchi are popular in northern Italian regions, where pumpkins grow in abundance during the fall. You can use whichever edible pumpkin you can find, or butternut squash works well, too. The only danger is, once you start to eat these gnocchi, you will want more and more!

SERVES 4

1 lb 2 oz (500 g) whole pumpkin (12 oz/350 g prepped weight)
12 oz (350 g) potatoes suitable for mashing, peeled and cut into chunks
1 egg
7 oz (200 g) all-purpose flour, plus extra for dusting
pinch of grated nutmeg
sea salt and freshly ground black pepper

For the sauce
5½ tbsp (80 g) butter
6 small rosemary sprigs
3 tbsp grated Parmesan

Preheat the oven to 400°F (200°C).

Peel the pumpkin and cut into chunks or slices (discarding the seeds). Place on a baking sheet and roast in the oven for 25–30 minutes, until cooked through and tender.

Meanwhile, bring a pot of salted water to a boil and cook the potato chunks until tender, then steam-dry. Mash the potatoes and pumpkin separately, then combine.

Add the egg, flour, and a pinch of nutmeg to the mash, season to taste, and mix until you obtain a smooth, soft dough, then leave to rest for about 10 minutes.

On a lightly floured work surface, roll the dough out into a long sausage shape. Using a sharp knife, cut into ¾ in (2 cm) lengths. Continue doing this until all the dough has been used.

Bring a large pot of salted water to a boil and drop the gnocchi into the water in batches, simmering for a minute or so until they rise to the top.

Meanwhile, make the sauce. Melt the butter in a large frying pan with the rosemary sprigs. As the gnocchi rise to the top, lift them out with a slotted spoon or spider strainer and transfer them to the pan with the butter and rosemary, mixing well together but taking care not to break the gnocchi. Sprinkle with the Parmesan and serve immediately.

ZUPPA DI ZUCCA E RICOTTA CON FUNGHI SALTATI

Pumpkin and ricotta soup with sautéed mushrooms

This perfect winter warmer is ideal to make during the cooler months when pumpkins are plentiful. Use whatever pumpkin you can find or, of course, butternut squash would be perfect, too. The addition of ricotta brings extra creaminess to this blended soup and the sautéed mushrooms add a lovely contrasting texture, as well as extra nutrition. I like to use a little guanciale for extra flavor but you could use pancetta or bacon, or simply omit it, if making for vegetarians.

SERVES 4

approx. 2 lb 4 oz (1 kg) whole pumpkin
¼ cup (60 ml) extra virgin olive oil
2 garlic cloves, left whole and squashed
1 red chile, finely sliced (optional)
3½ oz (100 g) guanciale (pork cheek), chopped into small cubes
leaves of 2 thyme sprigs, plus extra leaves to garnish
5 cups (1.2 liters) hot vegetable stock
7 oz (200 g) chestnut mushrooms, finely sliced
⅔ cup (150 g) ricotta
sea salt and freshly ground black pepper

Remove the skin and seeds from the pumpkin and chop the flesh into chunks, then set aside.

Heat 3 tablespoons of the olive oil in a large pot over medium-high heat and sweat the garlic, chile (if using), and half of the guanciale until the guanciale begins to color. Discard the garlic, then stir in the pumpkin and thyme. Pour in the hot stock, bring to a boil, then reduce the heat and simmer, partially covered with a lid, for about 25 minutes until the pumpkin is cooked through.

In the meantime, heat the remaining olive oil in a frying pan over medium-high heat and stir-fry the remaining guanciale until crispy. Add the mushrooms, season to taste, then continue to stir-fry for a couple of minutes until the mushrooms are cooked through.

Blend the pumpkin mixture until smooth, then check for seasoning and stir in the ricotta. Divide the soup among four bowls, top with the guanciale and mushroom mixture, garnish with extra thyme leaves, and serve immediately.

INSALATA TIEPIDA DI ZUCCA
Warm *pumpkin* salad

Pumpkin, combined with sweet roasted red onions, dried fruit, and pomegranate seeds, makes the perfect winter salad and is delicious eaten warm or cold. I recommend you use the Delica or Kabocha pumpkin for their sweet, delicate flavor, plus you can also eat the roasted skin, so nothing is wasted. If you can't find ricotta salata, use feta cheese.

SERVES 4

approx. 2 lb (900 g) whole pumpkin or squash
¼ cup (60 ml) extra virgin olive oil
4 small rosemary sprigs
3 red onions, cut into quarters
3½ oz (100 g) watercress
¼ cup (40 g) golden or brown raisins, soaked in a little warm water to soften
seeds of 1 pomegranate
1 oz (30 g) ricotta salata, crumbled or grated
sea salt and freshly ground black pepper

For the dressing
¼ cup (60 ml) extra virgin olive oil
2 tbsp white wine vinegar
a few rosemary needles, finely chopped
sea salt and freshly ground black pepper

Preheat the oven to 425°F (220°C).

Cut the pumpkin into ¾ in (2 cm) thick slices (leaving the skin on but discarding the seeds), then place in a roasting pan. Combine the olive oil with some salt and pepper and brush about half of this mixture over each pumpkin slice and scatter over the needles of two rosemary sprigs.

Place the onion quarters in another roasting pan, drizzle over the remaining olive oil mixture, and scatter over the remaining rosemary, then roast in the oven for about 40 minutes, until cooked through and turning golden brown. After 20 minutes, place the pumpkin in the oven and roast for about 20 minutes until cooked through and also turning golden brown.

Meanwhile, combine all the dressing ingredients in a jug and whisk until slightly thickened.

Place the watercress in a large serving dish, arrange the roasted pumpkin and onions over the top, and scatter over the raisins, pomegranate seeds, and ricotta salata. Pour over the dressing and serve immediately.

Eggplants
Beets
Radicchio
Red Cabbage

PURPLE VEGETABLES

EGGPLANTS
MELANZANE

Originating in Southeast Asia and first brought to Sicily by the Arabs, eggplants are now so widely grown and universally loved by Italians that this vegetable should really be the symbol of southern Italy. It is therefore strange to think that they were once viewed as poisonous—some said they caused madness, hence the Italian name *melanzana,* from the words *mela* (apple) and *insana* (insane), meaning insane apple! However, over time, eggplants were put to good use in the Italian kitchen and became the basis of many southern specialties, like the famous *Parmigiana alla Melanzane* (see page 198).

Mainly grown in Sicily and other southern Italian regions, eggplants come in many different shapes and sizes, from large and round, to oval, long, and miniature. The most common is the oval-shaped variety that is almost black in color, but Italy also produces beautiful stripy, pale purple and even white eggplants, as well as *Barbarella*, which is very round and richly purple, and native to Sicily.

Although referred to as a vegetable and cooked like one, eggplants are actually a fruit, with edible seeds and a spongy white interior. It is this sponginess that makes eggplants so versatile in the kitchen as they can absorb flavors really well and also provide a meaty texture. Eggplants are often substituted for meat, especially in *cucina povera* dishes, and I even use them in place of steak (see page 203).

Cooking eggplants *al funghetto* is popular—frying small cubes with olive oil, garlic, and basil. They can be eaten as they are or added to tomato sauces or pasta dishes. *Caponata*, a sweet and sour Sicilian stew, mixes small cubes of fried eggplant with celery, tomato, olives, raisins, and pine nuts, and is often served as an appetizer with bread. Stuffed eggplants make a wonderfully satisfying main course, and sliced eggplants can easily be turned into an alternative pizza base (see page 204). I also like to mash their cooked flesh with garlic, breadcrumbs, grated cheese, and herbs, then shape into balls or patties and fry or oven-bake.

Italians love to pickle eggplants and my favorite method is to peel and thinly slice them, then place the raw flesh in a jar with salt and vinegar for a couple of hours, before draining and preserving them in extra virgin olive oil with garlic, red chile, and oregano. In Italy, we would always preserve eggplants towards the end of the summer, when they were plentiful, and fill our pantries with lots of jars in order to enjoy them all year round. They are lovely as part of an antipasto with cured meats and cheeses, or added to sandwiches and salads.

Eggplants can even be made into a dessert, like *Melanzane alla Cioccolata,* which is popular in my hometown on the Amalfi Coast. Eggplant slices are fried, dipped in chocolate, layered with ricotta and candied fruits, then chilled and traditionally enjoyed in mid-August, during the Italian holiday weekend of *ferragosto*.

How to use eggplants:

Buying and storing
Look for firm, glossy skin (avoid anything soft or blemished) and a fresh-looking green stalk. Store eggplants in a cool place in the kitchen and use them as soon as you can, otherwise store in the fridge for 2–3 days.

Preparing
In the past, people would sprinkle salt over eggplant slices before cooking them. This was to draw out the bitter juices, but with modern growing techniques, this is no longer necessary. It is also done to draw out the moisture and, as a result, the flesh becomes less absorbent and will no longer soak up oil while cooking.

Be careful when cooking eggplants as they do have a tendency to soak up a lot of oil when frying. Although they may become dry very quickly, don't be tempted to add more oil, simply reduce the heat and keep cooking gently. The eggplants will eventually exude their own liquid as well as the oil they initially absorbed.

LA PARMIGIANA DI MELANZANE
Traditional *eggplant* parmigiana

This is the traditional eggplant parmigiana that my family has been making for decades. It does take a little time to prepare but is so worth it, and it's great for making in advance and simply heating up when required. Parmigiana was always a side dish when I was growing up, but now I like to serve it as a main course, with a green or mixed salad on the side.

SERVES 6

1 lb 2 oz (500 g) eggplants, thinly sliced lengthways
all-purpose flour, for dusting
4 eggs
abundant sunflower or vegetable oil, for deep-frying
handful of basil leaves
2¼ oz (65 g) Parmesan, grated
1 x 4½ oz (125 g) ball of mozzarella cheese, drained and thinly sliced
sea salt and freshly ground black pepper
mixed green salad, to serve

For the tomato sauce
2 tbsp extra virgin olive oil
½ onion, finely chopped
1 small garlic clove, squashed and left whole
2 x 14 oz (400 g) cans chopped tomatoes or jars tomato passata
sea salt

Place the eggplant slices in a dish, sprinkle with salt, cover with parchment paper, and place a weight on top (this can be some cans of beans or whatever else you have on hand), then set aside for 30 minutes (see Tip opposite).

Meanwhile, prepare the tomato sauce. Heat the olive oil in a sauté pan over medium heat and sweat the onion and garlic for a couple of minutes until softened. Stir in the tomatoes with about half a can of water and a little salt to taste and simmer over medium-low heat for about 25 minutes. Discard the garlic clove.

Preheat the oven to 400°F (200°C).

Place a clean kitchen towel on a work surface, arrange the salted eggplant slices in a single layer on top, then cover with another clean kitchen towel and pat dry, ensuring all the eggplants are as dry as possible.

Spread a little flour over the surface of a medium-sized plate and, in a shallow, wide bowl, beat the eggs with a little salt. Coat the eggplant slices, first in a little flour, shaking off any excess, then in the beaten egg.

Heat plenty of oil in a large, deep frying pan until hot, then deep-fry the coated eggplant slices in batches for a couple of minutes on each side until golden. Using a slotted spoon, transfer to paper towels to drain and pat dry with more paper to remove as much excess oil as possible.

Line a baking dish (approx. 7 in by 9½ in/18 cm x 24 cm) with a little of the tomato sauce, arrange a layer of eggplants on top, and scatter with some basil leaves, followed by a sprinkling of grated Parmesan, some mozzarella, and a twist of black pepper. Continue making layers like these until you finish all the ingredients, ending with tomato sauce and grated Parmesan.

Cover with foil and bake in the oven for 20 minutes, then remove the foil and continue to bake for a further 20 minutes, until the top is a nice golden brown color.

Remove from the oven, leave to rest for 5–10 minutes, then slice and serve with a salad.

Keep in the fridge for up to 2 days.

TIP
Sprinkling the eggplant slices with salt and leaving them with a weight on top will help exude a lot of the moisture and avoid unnecessary liquid in the finished dish.

PASTA 'NSCIATA
Eggplant pasta bake

This hearty pasta bake is a classic from Sicily. It can be made in many different ways but always includes eggplants, local *caciocavallo* cheese, and cured meat. This richer version includes a ground beef ragù and is typically eaten in the Messina area of the island—it actually gets a mention on the popular Italian detective TV drama *Montalbano* as being his favorite meal!

As *caciocavallo* isn't widely available, I have used provolone picante instead, but you can always substitute a strong Cheddar, if you prefer, and swap the mortadella for cooked ham or a mixture of salami. A simple tomato sauce is also delicious, instead of a ragù.

SERVES 4–6

abundant vegetable oil, for frying
1 eggplant (approx 9 oz/250 g), thinly sliced lengthways
10½ oz (300 g) rigatoni or tortiglioni pasta
a little butter, for greasing
1 tbsp dried breadcrumbs, for dusting
1¾ oz (50 g) provolone picante cheese, cut into small cubes
2 cold hard-boiled eggs, peeled and sliced into rounds
1 x 4½ oz (125 g) ball of mozzarella cheese, drained and roughly chopped
1¾ oz (50 g) mortadella, roughly chopped
¼ cup (30 g) grated Parmesan
handful of basil leaves, plus extra to garnish
sea salt and freshly ground black pepper

For the ragù
1 tbsp extra virgin olive oil
½ onion, finely chopped
½ celery stalk, finely chopped
½ carrot, finely chopped
9 oz (250 g) ground beef
2 tbsp white wine
1½ cups (350 ml) tomato passata
sea salt and freshly ground black pepper

First make the ragù. Heat the olive oil in a heavy-based pot over medium heat and sweat the onion, celery, and carrot for a couple of minutes until softened. Increase the heat, add the ground beef, and sear well all over, then season with salt and pepper. Add the wine and allow to evaporate. Add the tomato passata, lower the heat, partially cover with a lid, and cook gently for 1½ hours. If the sauce gets a little too thick during cooking, add a little hot water.

Meanwhile, heat plenty of vegetable oil in a large, deep frying pan until hot, then deep-fry the eggplant slices in batches for 2–3 minutes until golden all over. Using a slotted spoon, transfer to paper towels to drain and pat dry with more paper to remove as much excess oil as possible. Set aside.

Preheat the oven to 400°F (200°C).

Bring a large pot of salted water to a boil and cook the rigatoni until al dente. Drain and combine with a ladleful of the ragù mixture.

Lightly grease a baking dish (7 in x 11 in/18 cm x 28 cm) with butter and dust with breadcrumbs. Spread about a third of the ragù over the top, followed by half of the cooked pasta. Scatter over half of the provolone, egg slices, mozzarella, and mortadella, plus a sprinkling of grated Parmesan, then layer half of the eggplant slices on top. Spread half of the remaining ragù on top, with a scatter of some basil leaves and a little black pepper, then add the remaining pasta, provolone, egg slices, mozzarella, mortadella, grated Parmesan, and eggplant slices as before. Scatter with more basil leaves and finish with a layer of the remaining ragù.

Cover the dish with foil and bake in the oven for 20 minutes, then remove the foil and continue to bake for a further 15 minutes, until hot and bubbling.

Remove from the oven, leave to rest for 5 minutes, then serve.

"BISTECCHE" DI MELANZANA
Eggplant "steaks"

Eggplants are quite "meaty" in texture so are perfect as pretend steaks! You can simply brush them with a little oil and grill them, but my preference is to dip them in beaten egg and coat them in breadcrumbs before frying them—a much tastier option. Serve with a tomato salad with basil gremolata and lots of rustic bread.

SERVES 2

2 eggs
½ cup (50 g) dried breadcrumbs
¼ cup (30 g) grated Parmesan
1 eggplant (approx. 10½ oz/300 g), sliced lengthways into approx. ¼ in (5 mm) thick slices
all-purpose flour, for coating
abundant vegetable or sunflower oil, for deep-frying
14 oz (400 g) small tomatoes, thinly sliced
1 small red onion, thinly sliced
a few arugula leaves
sea salt and freshly ground black pepper

For the basil gremolata
½ handful of basil leaves, finely chopped
zest of ½ lemon
1 small garlic clove, finely diced
2½ tbsp extra virgin olive oil
pinch of sea salt

First make the basil gremolata by combining all the ingredients together in a bowl, then set aside.

In a shallow bowl, lightly beat the eggs with a little salt and pepper. In another bowl, combine the breadcrumbs and grated Parmesan.

Coat the eggplant slices in flour, shaking off the excess, then dip first into the beaten egg and then coat in the breadcrumb mixture.

Heat plenty of cooking oil in a large, deep frying pan over medium heat until hot, then deep-fry the eggplant slices a couple at a time (depending on the size of your pan) for about 3 minutes on each side until golden. Using a slotted spoon, transfer to paper towels to drain and pat dry with more paper to remove as much excess oil as possible.

Arrange the eggplant slices on plates and top with the basil gremolata. Serve with tomato, red onion, and arugula alongside.

Purple Vegetables

"PIZZETTE" DI MELANZANE
Eggplant "pizzette"

Although these aren't quite mini pizzas (with eggplant slices for a base), they do look a bit like them and are ideal for parties or for a light meal, served with a green salad. Try and find a large round eggplant as this will give you ideal-sized slices. If you can only find the more common oval-shaped eggplants, you will probably need to use two.

MAKES 10–12 SLICES

1 large round purple eggplant (approx. 1 lb 2 oz/500 g)
2 tbsp extra virgin olive oil, plus extra for brushing and drizzling
1 garlic clove, smashed
10½ oz (300 g) baby plum tomatoes, cut in half
2 tsp capers
15 pitted black olives
1 x 4½ oz (125 g) ball of mozzarella cheese, drained and roughly chopped
sea salt
10–12 basil leaves, to garnish

Preheat the oven to 425°F (220°C).

Cut the eggplant widthways into just under ½ in (1 cm) thick slices, then prick all over with a fork and lightly brush both sides with a little olive oil. Arrange the slices in a single layer on a large baking sheet lined with parchment paper and bake in the oven for 10 minutes, turning the slices over halfway through for even cooking.

Meanwhile, heat the olive oil in a frying pan over low heat and fry the garlic for a minute, then add the tomatoes, capers, and olives with a little salt, turn up the heat to medium-high, and stir-fry for about 5 minutes, until the tomatoes have softened but are not mushy. Discard the garlic.

Remove the eggplant slices from the oven and top each one with a little of the tomato sauce and mozzarella. Bake in the oven for 7–8 minutes, until the mozzarella has melted.

Remove from the oven and serve with a basil leaf on top of each.

BEETS
BARBABIETOLA

When thinking of Italian vegetables, beet is probably not one of the first that comes to mind. However, this dark red root vegetable certainly has a place in the Italian kitchen and, nutritionally speaking, is also very good for you—packed with vitamins and minerals, especially iron, and associated with lowering high blood pressure.

The first beets were originally grown for their leaves in the ancient Middle East and it was not until the Roman era that the roots began to be consumed. They were viewed as medicinal and used to treat digestive and blood conditions.

Beets are easy to grow and harvests from the end of summer through to fall/winter. They are mainly grown in northern Italy and there is one particular variety that Italy prides itself on—the *Chioggia*, with its light red skin and beautiful candy-striped pink and white interior. This mild-tasting beet from the region around Venice is quite a delicacy and often not easily obtainable.

In Italian cooking, beet is traditionally used in salads. However, it has recently become trendy in restaurant cooking, especially for its vibrant juices, which are used to color pasta, risotto (see page 208), and gnocchi and has lots of potential for presentation.

Beet is commonly pickled and I remember this from when I was a child in Italy. My mother would always have jars of it at home and we would add it to salads or simply enjoy as a snack with bread. It is incredibly versatile and is delicious boiled, roasted, blended in a soup, drunk as a juice, used as a filling for ravioli, or even as a pesto. It marries exceptionally well with strong cheeses like Taleggio, Gorgonzola, and goat cheese, as well as oranges—I often combine the two in a deliciously sweet salad. Because of its sweetness, beet is also often used in cakes, cookies, and other sweet treats.

You can buy packages of plain pre-cooked beets and these are fine, but I prefer to buy them fresh in bunches from the market in season. If you're lucky, in addition to the purple variety, you can find different colored beets in white, orange, and pinks.

How to use beets:

Buying and storing
Look for firm roots and fresh-looking stalks and leaves. The roots will keep in a cool, dark place, maybe in the same place you keep your potatoes, for a few days.

Preparing
Wash the beets but don't peel, leave the roots at the bottom (otherwise the juices will leech and stain) and chop the stalks to about 1 in (2.5 cm). Bring a pot of salted water to a boil, add the beets, and simmer for about an hour (depending on size), until cooked through, then drain.

When cool enough to handle, remove the skins, which should come off easily. Slice and combine with olive oil and a sprinkling of sea salt and chopped flat-leaf parsley, or use in other dishes. Cooked beets can be stored in the fridge for up to 3 days.

If the leaves are fresh-looking, use them as you would chard or spinach (they are closely related) and add them to salads, soups, and stir-fries. However, use them quickly as they tend to turn yellow quite quickly. The roots have a much longer shelf-life.

You can also eat beets raw, either very finely sliced as a carpaccio (see page 211), or grated into salads and slaws.

The only downside with cooked beets is that, once the skin is off, they stain everything they comes into contact with—work surfaces, plates, your hands and clothes—so take care when handling.

RISOTTO ALLA BARBABIETOLA E DOLCELATTE
Beet risotto with dolcelatte cheese

This rich-colored risotto oozes with creaminess from the dolcelatte cheese, which combines perfectly with the earthy flavor of the beets. It would certainly impress guests at a dinner party and makes a comforting family meal at any time. Dolcelatte cheese can be substituted for Gorgonzola.

SERVES 4

9 oz (250 g) raw beets
approx. 7½ cups (1.8 liters) hot vegetable stock
2 tbsp extra virgin olive oil, plus extra for drizzling
2 tbsp butter
1 banana shallot, finely chopped
1¼ cups (250 g) arborio rice
scant ½ cup (100 ml) white wine
3 oz (80 g) dolcelatte or Gorgonzola cheese, roughly chopped, plus extra to garnish
sea salt
finely chopped flat-leaf parsley, to garnish

Bring a pot of salted water to a boil and cook the raw beets for about 50 minutes until tender and cooked through. Drain, leave to cool, then peel off the skins. Roughly chop, then transfer to a blender and blend with a couple of tablespoons of the hot stock and a drizzle of olive oil. Set aside.

Heat the olive oil and butter in a heavy-based pot over medium heat and sweat the shallot for a minute or so until softened. Stir in the rice until each grain is coated in the oil.

Add the wine, stir, and allow to evaporate. Add a ladle or two of hot stock and stir with a wooden spoon until the rice has absorbed the liquid.

Continue adding the stock and cooking like this for about 15–17 minutes until the rice is cooked al dente. Stir in the blended beets, mixing well. Remove from the heat and beat in the cheese.

Serve immediately with small dollops of dolcelatte and a sprinkling of chopped parsley.

CARPACCIO DI BARBABIETOLE
Beet carpaccio

The secret to this salad is to slice the beets incredibly thinly so the acidity of the lemon juice will "cook" them. However, if you prefer to roast the beets, there is no need to marinate it in this way. Serve with rustic bread for a light summery lunch or appetizer.

SERVES 4

13 oz (375 g) raw beets, washed and skin scrubbed
juice of 1 lemon
3 tbsp extra virgin olive oil
1 tbsp balsamic vinegar
2 oz (60 g) arugula
Parmesan shavings
zest of ½ orange
sea salt

Using a mandolin or a sharp knife, slice the beets into very thin slivers. Arrange the slices in a large dish, pour over the lemon juice, and leave to marinate for about 30 minutes.

In a small jug, combine the olive oil and balsamic vinegar with a little salt.

Top the beets with the arugula leaves, drizzle over the dressing, and finish with a scatter of Parmesan shavings and orange zest.

RADICCHIO
RADICCHIO

If there is one thing to look forward to in winter, it has to be the vibrant wine-red radicchio leaf, which will brighten up any kitchen and plate.

Belonging to the chicory family, radicchio (from the Latin *radiculus,* meaning root), is the Italian name for several varieties that are grown in the Veneto area of northern Italy. The most popular and widely available is the *Radicchio di Chioggia*, a round head of leaves that can easily be mistaken for red cabbage. This is also the type that is most commonly found in supermarkets.

The *Radicchio Rosso di Treviso*, a variety that has been around since the sixteenth century, is a elongated with pointed red leaves, a crunchy white stem, and a closed, fairly compact appearance. Grown in open fields, the production is quite labor-intensive and it's not easily available outside Italy, except perhaps in specialist grocery stores at a price. The *Radicchio Rosso di Treviso Tardivo* has a slightly later season, and is comprised of tightly clustered bunches of long slender leaves, which curl inwards at the top. Like the *Treviso*, the *Tardivo* is labor-intensive; harvested by hand and then tied into bunches, and stored in a dark environment with the bases soaked in local spring water for blanching. The result is a white stem with white and dark red-purple leaves; you'd almost be tempted to put them in a vase like flowers. The *Tardivo* has been given IGP status.

The other variety is *Radicchio di Castelfranco*, a pretty round-shaped yellow lettuce with red speckled flecks all over. Again, almost too pretty to eat, it is often known as *rosa d'inverno* (winter rose and has protected IGP status.

The radicchio varieties may look different but they all have a characteristic bitter taste that goes well with sweet ingredients and citrusy flavors, which Italians love. They are often added to winter salads (with fennel and orange) or served alongside strong cheeses like Gorgonzola, with ripe pears, walnuts, and balsamic vinegar.

Cooking helps to take away some of radicchio's bitterness and grilling is a popular way to cook chicory, by cutting it into quarters and placing it over a hot grill. Roasted radicchio, with a mix of breadcrumbs, Parmesan, herbs, and olive oil, is delicious as a side dish. Chopped radicchio heads are also used in risotto dishes, as a filling for ravioli or savory pies and tarts, as well as in cheesy soufflés and *sformato* (see page 213).

The pretty leaves of the *Tardivo* make a lovely addition to the Italian crudité dish, *Pinzimonio*, where raw vegetables are dipped into olive oil and salt.

How to use radicchio:

Buying and storing
Look for compact heads and fresh leaves without blemishes or bruising. Store in the salad drawer of the fridge, where it should last a week (but the *Castelfranco* only 2 days).

Preparing
When preparing radicchio in chunks to be baked or grilled, don't remove the core or the leaves will fall apart. If slicing for salads or cooked dishes, remove the core and slice the leaves.

SFORMATO DI RADICCHIO
Cheesy *radicchio* terrine

Despite the quantity of cheese, this is a surprisingly light dish and the slight bitterness of radicchio tends to disappear once it is cooked. Serve with a crisp green salad.

SERVES 4

5¾ oz (160 g) radicchio leaves
½ tbsp white wine vinegar
10½ oz (300 g) potatoes, any kind suitable for mashing, peeled and chopped
2 tbsp extra virgin olive oil
½ tbsp white wine
2½ oz (70 g) provolone picante cheese, grated
¼ cup (25 g) grated Parmesan
1 egg
½ cup (125 g) ricotta
sea salt and freshly ground black pepper

Preheat the oven to 400°F (200°C) and line a 9 in x 5½ in (900 g) loaf pan with parchment paper.

Take the radicchio and set aside 2 oz (60 g) of the largest leaves. In a pot, combine the vinegar with some water and a pinch of salt and blanch the radicchio leaves for a minute. Remove and drain on a clean kitchen towel, placing another kitchen towel over the top to pat dry.

Bring a pot of salted water to a boil and cook the potatoes until tender, then drain and steam-dry.

Finely slice the remaining radicchio leaves. Heat the olive oil in a small frying pan, add the sliced radicchio, and stir-fry over medium-high heat for 2–3 minutes. Add the white wine and allow to evaporate, then remove from the heat and leave to cool.

Line the prepared loaf pan with about three-quarters of the blanched radicchio leaves, ensuring you cover all the bottom and allow the leaves to overlap the edge.

Mash the cooked potatoes and combine with the provolone, Parmesan, egg, ricotta, and cooked radicchio. Season with black pepper.

Fill the loaf pan with this mixture and cover with the overlapping radicchio leaves, then place the remaining leaves over the top to cover any gaps. Cover with foil, bake in the oven for 55 minutes, then remove the foil and continue to bake for a further 5 minutes.

Remove from the oven, leave to rest for 5 minutes, then remove from the pan, slice, and serve.

PASTA CON RADICCHIO E GORGONZOLA
Pasta with *radicchio* and creamy Gorgonzola

Radicchio and Gorgonzola make a perfect match and this nutritious dish is a must during the winter months when radicchio is widely available. Use the pasta cooking water to wilt the radicchio leaves, as well as to turn the Gorgonzola nice and creamy. The addition of walnuts at the end brings a nice crunchy contrast.

SERVES 4

14 oz (400 g) penne lisce
3 tbsp extra virgin olive oil
1 large onion, finely chopped
9 oz (250 g) radicchio leaves, finely chopped
7 oz (200 g) Gorgonzola cheese, roughly cut into cubes
12 walnut halves, broken into pieces
sea salt and freshly ground black pepper

Bring a large pot of salted water to a boil and cook the pasta until al dente.

Meanwhile, heat the olive oil in a large frying pan over medium heat and sweat the onion for about 5 minutes until softened. Stir in the radicchio, season to taste, and stir-fry for a minute, then add a couple of tablespoons of the hot pasta cooking water, cover with a lid, and cook for about 5 minutes, until the radicchio is tender.

Stir in the Gorgonzola with about 4 tablespoons of hot pasta cooking water, mixing well to obtain a creamy consistency. Drain the pasta, add to the sauce, increase the heat, and cook for a minute to mix well together.

Serve immediately with a sprinkling of black pepper and a scattering of walnuts.

INSALATA DI RADICCHIO, CECI E GORZONZOLA

Radicchio, chickpea, and Gorgonzola salad

This perfect winter salad uses some of my favorite ingredients. The slightly bitter taste of radicchio marries perfectly with juicy sweet pears and creamy Gorgonzola, and the addition of chickpeas brings more texture and makes it a little more filling. I love chestnuts but, if you prefer, you can replace them with walnuts.

SERVES 4

1 radicchio head
2 ripe Bosc pears
1 x 14 oz (400 g) can chickpeas, drained and rinsed
8 cooked (shelled) chestnuts, sliced in halves or quarters (depending on size)
3 oz (80 g) Gorgonzola cheese, roughly chopped
2 tbsp extra virgin olive oil
1 tbsp balsamic vinegar
sea salt and freshly ground black pepper

Remove the leaves of the radicchio head and chop the large ones in half, keeping the smaller ones intact. Core the pears and cut into slices.

Place the radicchio leaves, pear slices, chickpeas, chestnuts, and Gorgonzola in a large bowl. Combine the olive oil and balsamic vinegar in a jug, season with salt and pepper, then pour over the salad, tossing well to coat.

Arrange on a serving dish and serve immediately.

Red Cabbage
CAVOLO ROSSO

The *rosso*, sometimes known as *Cavolo Cappuccio Rosso*, is a red cabbage that is also grown in the northeast of Italy. It is often slow-cooked with sugar, spices, apples, and a little vinegar, and makes a wonderful accompaniment to meat and game dishes. The wonderful deep purple of the cabbage also makes a beautiful risotto, or it can be blended into a creamy soup, added to pasta, or thinly sliced in salads and pickles.

How to prepare *red cabbage*:

When buying rosso, look for firm, heavy heads and keep stored in a cool, dark place in the kitchen. It keeps for longer than the green Savoy cabbage and can last for over a week in the fridge.

AGRODOLCE DI CAVOLO ROSSO
Sweet and sour *red cabbage*

This makes the perfect accompaniment to roast meats and is delicious eaten hot or cold. It can be made in advance and stored in the fridge for up to four days and, in fact, the longer you leave it, the tastier it becomes as the flavors have time to infuse. If you do make it in advance, add the parsley and orange zest just before serving.

SERVES 6–8

1 red cabbage (approx. 1 lb 12 oz/ 800 g)
4½ tbsp white wine or cider vinegar
2½ tsp sugar, any type
2 tbsp extra virgin olive oil
2 garlic cloves, left whole and squashed
3 tbsp raisins
3 tbsp pine nuts
½ handful of flat-leaf parsley, finely chopped
zest of 1 orange
sea salt and freshly ground black pepper

Remove and discard the tough outer leaves of the red cabbage and the tough bits inside, then finely slice.

In a bowl or jug, combine the vinegar and sugar, then set aside.

Heat the olive oil in a large pot over medium heat and sweat the garlic cloves for a minute or so to flavor the oil. Discard the garlic cloves. Add the raisins and pine nuts and stir-fry for a minute, then add the red cabbage and stir-fry for a further minute. Reduce the heat, season with a little salt and pepper, cover with a lid, and cook over a gentle heat for 30 minutes.

Stir in the vinegar and sugar mixture and continue to cook, uncovered, over medium heat for 15 minutes.

Remove from the heat, sprinkle with the parsley and orange zest, and serve.

TIP
Keep in the fridge for up to 3 days.

INDEX

agrodolce di cavolo rosso 219
almonds: carrot and almond cake 148
anchovies
    Belgian endive salad 141
    broccoli cooked in red wine with provolone cheese 34
    fennel "steaks" served with an orange salad 67
    Ligurian-style rainbow chard frittata 123
    pizza with scamorza and arugula 87
    trofie pasta with puntarelle 96
Antonella's fried zucchinis 53
arancini di funghi 160
artichokes 8–9
    artichoke pâté 13
    artichokes with peas and fava beans 28
    baked filled artichokes 12
    tuna-filled artichoke hearts 11
arugula 86
    arugula tart 90
    beet carpaccio 211
    pizza with scamorza and arugula 87
    risotto with arugula and taleggio cheese 89
asparagi alla valdostana 18
asparagus 16–17
    baked cheesy asparagus 18
    pasta with asparagus carbonara 23
    savory asparagus tart 20

barbabietola 206–207
beef: eggplant pasta bake 200–201
beets 206–207
    beet carpaccio 211
    beet risotto with dolcelatte cheese 208
Belgian endives 92, 140, 212
    Belgian endive salad 141
    filled Belgian endive 142
bietole 118
"bistecche" di melanzana 203
bread
    baked caprese "salad' 134
    baked filled artichokes 12
    crispy potato "focaccia" 178
    eggplant "steaks" 203
    fennel "steaks" served with an orange salad 67
    filled baked mushrooms 165
    filled flatbread from Emilia Romangna 124
    filled zucchinis 55
    lettuce and watercress soup 93
    pea polpette served with a spicy tomato sauce 82
    peppers with breadcrumbs 112
    puntarelle and bread salad 95
    sweet chard tart 120

broccoli 30
    broccoli cooked in red wine with provolone cheese 34
    broccoli fritters 32
    cheesy broccoli soup 31
broccoli alla Siciliana 34

cabbage 36–37
    cabbage soup 39
    cabbage strudel with baked ricotta 41
    stuffed cabbage leaves in tomato sauce 38
    sweet and sour red cabbage 219
cakes
    carrot and almond cake 148
    sweet potato and chocolate loaf cake 174
    zucchini cake 61
cannellini beans: leek and cannellini bean soup 75
capers
    Belgian endive salad 141
    eggplant "pizzette" 204
    fennel "steaks" served with an orange salad 67
    leeks agrodolce (sweet and sour) 77
    peppers with breadcrumbs 112
    pizza with scamorza and arugula 87
    potato bake with tomatoes and capers 173
    trofie pasta with puntarelle 96
    tuna-filled artichoke hearts 11
caprese al forno 134
carbonara di asparagi 23
carciofi 8–9
carciofi ripieni al forno 12
carpaccio di barbabietola 211
carrots/carote 144–151
    cabbage soup 39
    carrot and almond cake 148
    carrot soufflés with parsley sauce 150
    roasted carrot and parsnip soup 146
    stuffed cabbage leaves in tomato sauce 38
    eggplant pasta bake 200–201
cauliflower 148
    mashed cauliflower bake 149
    cauliflower "polpette" 154
    Italian cauliflower cheese with mushrooms 157
cavolfiore 148
cavolfiore al forno con funghi e formaggio 157
cavolo 36–37
cavolo rosso 218
celery 42–43
    baked celery with onions and black olives 46
    cabbage soup 39
    celery pasta salad 49

celery pesto 44
eggplant pasta bake 200–201
stuffed cabbage leaves in tomato sauce 38
chard 118
    filled flatbread from Emilia Romangna 124
    Ligurian-style rainbow chard frittata 123
    sweet chard tart 120
cheese
    arugula tart 90
    baked caprese "salad" 134
    baked cheesy asparagus 18
    beet risotto with dolcelatte cheese 208
    broccoli cooked in red wine with provolone cheese 34
    cabbage strudel with baked ricotta 41
    carrot soufflés with parsley sauce 150
    cauliflower "polpette" 154
    celery pasta salad 49
    celery pesto 44
    cheesy broccoli soup 31
    cheesy radicchio terrine 213
    cheesy spinach "terrine" 105
    eggplant pasta bake 200–201
    eggplant "pizzette" 204
    eggplant "steaks" 203
    fennel soup 64
    filled baked mushrooms 165
    filled zucchini flowers 58
    filled zucchinis 55
    filled flatbread from Emilia Romangna 124
    filled mushroom balls 160
    filled peppers 113
    green bean bake 72
    Italian cauliflower cheese with mushrooms 157
    Italian-style baked potatoes 183
    leek and cannellini bean soup 75
    mashed cauliflower bake 153
    Neopolitan potato croquettes 177
    onion pie 170
    pasta with radicchio and creamy Gorgonzola 215
    pea polpette served with a spicy tomato sauce 82
    pea soufflés 85
    penne with creamy roasted pepper sauce 114
    peppers with breadcrumbs 112
    pizza with scamorza and arugula 87
    polenta lasagne with mushrooms 163–164
    pumpkin and ricotta soup with sautéed mushrooms 187
    radicchio, chickpea, and Gorgonzola salad 216

risotto with arugula and taleggio cheese 89
savory asparagus tart 20
spaghetti with fava beans and pecorino 27
spinach gnocchi 102
spinach lasagne 101
traditional eggplant parmigiana 198–199
warm pumpkin salad 190
zucchini saltimbocca 54
chestnuts: radicchio, chickpea, and Gorgonzola salad 216
chickpeas: radicchio, chickpea, and Gorgonzola salad 216
chocolate: sweet potato and chocolate loaf cake 174
cipolle 166–167
cipolotti 166
crema di carciofi 13
crema di carote e pastinaca arrostite 146
crescione romagnolo 124
crocantella di patate 178

eggs
   arugula tart 90
   baked cheesy asparagus 18
   carrot soufflés with parsley sauce 150
   eggplant pasta bake 200–201
   Ligurian-style rainbow chard frittata 123
   Neopolitan potato croquettes 177
   onion pie 170
   pasta with asparagus carbonara 23
   pea soufflés 85
   puntarelle and bread salad 95
   savory asparagus tart 20
eggplants 196–197
   eggplant pasta bake 200–201
   eggplant "pizzette" 204
   eggplant "steaks" 203
   traditional eggplant parmigiana 198–199
endivia belga 140
endivia belga ripiena 142

fagiolini 68–69
fagiolini alla pizzaiola 70
fava beans 24–25
   artichokes with peas and fava beans 28
   spaghetti with fava beans and pecorino 27
   split fava bean stew 26
favata 26
fave 24–25
fennel 62–63
   fennel cooked in milk 65
   fennel soup 64
   fennel "steaks" served with an orange salad 67
   split fava bean stew 26
finocchi al latte 65
finocchi impanati con insalata d'arance 67

finocchio 62–63
fiori di zucca ripieni 58
fish *see also* anchovies
   tuna-filled artichoke hearts 11
foglie di cavolo ripiene con salsa al pomodoro 38
fondo di carciofi al tonno 11
frittelle di broccoli 32
frittata di bietole alla ligure 123
frittedda siciliana 28
funghi 158–159
funghi ripieni al forno 165

gatto' di cavolfiore 153
gnocchi di spinaci 102
gnocchi di zucca 186
green beans 68–69
   green bean bake 72
   green beans with tomatoes 70
guanciale: pumpkin and ricotta soup with sautéed mushrooms 187

ham
   baked cheesy asparagus 18
   cabbage strudel with baked ricotta 41
   mashed cauliflower bake 153
   Italian-style baked potatoes 183
   savory asparagus tart 20
   zucchini saltimbocca 54
hazelnuts: zucchini cake 61

insalata di endivia belga 141
insalata di pasta al sedano 49
insalata di puntarelle e pane 95
insalata di radicchio, ceci e Gorgonzola 216
insalata tiepida di zucca 190
insalate 92

la genovese "scappata" con ziti 168
la parmigiana di melanzane 198–199
lasagne con spinaci 101
leeks 74
   cheesy broccoli soup 31
   leek and cannellini bean soup 75
   leeks agrodolce (sweet and sour) 77
   lettuce and watercress soup 93
lemons
   artichokes with peas and fava beans 28
   beet carpaccio 211
   celery pesto 44
   zucchini cake 61
lettuce and watercress soup 93
Ligurian-style rainbow chard frittata 123

melanzane 196–197
milk
   fennel cooked in milk 65
   filled zucchinis 55
   Italian cauliflower cheese with mushrooms 157

spinach lasagne 101
sweet chard tart 120
minestra di cavolo 39
mortadella: eggplant pasta bake 200–201
mushrooms 158–159
   filled baked mushrooms 165
   filled Belgian endive 142
   filled mushroom balls 160
   filled zucchinis 55
   Italian cauliflower cheese with mushrooms 157
   polenta lasagne with mushrooms 163–164
   pumpkin and ricotta soup with sautéed mushrooms 187

Neopolitan potato croquettes 177

olives
   baked caprese "salad" 134
   baked celery with onions and black olives 46
   broccoli cooked in red wine with provolone cheese 34
   eggplant "pizzette" 204
   fennel "steaks" served with an orange salad 67
   filled peppers 113
   leeks agrodolce (sweet and sour) 77
   onion pie 170
onions 166–167
   artichokes with peas and fava beans 28
   baked celery with onions and black olives 46
   cabbage soup 39
   cabbage strudel with baked ricotta 41
   crispy potato "focaccia" 178
   eggplant pasta bake 200–201
   fennel soup 64
   filled baked mushrooms 165
   leek and cannellini bean soup 75
   onion pie 170
   pasta with radicchio and creamy Gorgonzola 215
   potato bake with tomatoes and capers 173
   roasted carrot and parsnip soup 146
   split fava bean stew 26
   stewed peppers 110
   stuffed cabbage leaves in tomato sauce 38
   warm pumpkin salad 190
   ziti pasta with onions 168
oranges
   beet carpaccio 211
   fennel "steaks" served with an orange salad 67
   sweet and sour red cabbage 219

pancetta
   cabbage soup 39
   fennel soup 64
   leek and cannellini bean soup 75

pasta with asparagus carbonara 23
polenta lasagne with mushrooms 163–164
stuffed cabbage leaves in tomato sauce 38
panzarotti napoletani 177
parmigiana di melanzane 198–199
parsley: carrot soufflés with parsley sauce 150
parsnips 140
   roasted carrot and parsnip soup 146
pasta
   cabbage soup 39
   celery pasta salad 49
   eggplant pasta bake 200–201
   pasta with asparagus carbonara 23
   pasta with radicchio and creamy Gorgonzola 215
   penne with creamy roasted pepper sauce 114
   spaghetti with fava beans and pecorino 27
   spinach lasagne 101
   stuffed tomatoes 133
   trofie pasta with puntarelle 96
   ziti pasta with onions 168
pasta con radicchio e Gorgonzola 215
pasta 'nsciata 200–201
pasticcio di polenta e funghi 163–164
pastinaca 144, 146
patate 172
patate napoletane al forno 173
patate ripiene al forno 183
pears: radicchio, chickpea, and Gorgonzola salad 216
peas 78–79
   artichokes with peas and fava beans 28
   creamy pea and mint risotto 80
   pea polpette served with a spicy tomato sauce 82
   pea soufflés 85
penne con crema di peperoni arrostiti 114
peperonata 110
peperoni 108–109
peperoni alla mollica 112
peperoni ripieni 113
peppers 108–109
   filled peppers 113
   penne with creamy roasted pepper sauce 114
   peppers with breadcrumbs 112
   stewed peppers 110
pesto di sedano 44
pies
   cabbage strudel with baked ricotta 41
   onion pie 170
pine nuts
   Ligurian-style rainbow chard frittata 123
   sweet and sour red cabbage 219
piselli 78–79
pizza bianca con scamorza e rucola 87
pizza with scamorza and arugula 87
"pizzette" di melanzane 204
polenta: polenta lasagne with mushrooms 163–164

polpette di cavolfiore 154
polpette di piselli con salsa piccante al pomodoro 82
pomegranate: warm pumpkin salad 190
pomodori 128–129
pomodori ripieni di pasta 133
pork
   filled mushroom balls 160
   pumpkin and ricotta soup with sautéed mushrooms 187
   split fava bean stew 26
porri 74
porri all'agrodolce 77
potatoes 172
   baked filled artichokes 12
   cabbage soup 39
   cauliflower "polpette" 154
   cheesy broccoli soup 31
   cheesy radicchio terrine 213
   crispy potato "focaccia" 178
   fennel soup 64
   green bean bake 72
   Italian-style baked potatoes 183
   leek and cannellini bean soup 75
   lettuce and watercress soup 93
   mashed cauliflower bake 153
   Neopolitan potato croquettes 177
   potato bake with tomatoes and capers 173
   pumpkin gnocchi 186
   roasted carrot and parsnip soup 146
prosciutto: zucchini saltimbocca 54
pumpkin 184–185
   pumpkin and ricotta soup with sautéed mushrooms 187
   pumpkin gnocchi 186
   warm pumpkin salad 190
puntarelle 92
   puntarelle and bread salad 95
   trofie pasta with puntarelle 96

radicchio 212
   cheesy radicchio terrine 213
   pasta with radicchio and creamy Gorgonzola 215
   radicchio, chickpea, and Gorgonzola salad 216
raisins
   Ligurian-style rainbow chard frittata 123
   sweet and sour red cabbage 219
   sweet chard tart 120
   warm pumpkin salad 190
red cabbage 218
   sweet and sour red cabbage 219
rice
   beet risotto with dolcelatte cheese 208
   creamy pea and mint risotto 80
   risotto with arugula and Taleggio cheese 89
risotto alla barbabietola e dolcelatte 208
risotto con rucola e taleggio 89
risotto cremoso di piselli e menta 80
rucola 86

salad 92
   Belgian endive salad 141
   celery pasta salad 49
   fennel "steaks" served with an orange salad 67
   puntarelle and bread salad 95
   radicchio, chickpea, and Gorgonzola salad 216
   warm pumpkin salad 190
salami
   filled baked mushrooms 165
   Italian-style baked potatoes 183
salsa veloce di pomodorini 130
saltimbocca di zucchine 54
sausages: split fava bean stew 26
scalogni 166
sedano 42–43
sedano alla molisana 46
sformatini di carote con salsina verde 150
sformato de spinaci 105
sformato di fagiolini 72
sformato di radicchio 213
shallots 166
   pea soufflés 85
   spaghetti with fava beans and pecorino 27
sorbetto al pomodoro 136
soup
   cabbage soup 39
   cheesy broccoli soup 31
   fennel soup 64
   leek and cannellini bean soup 75
   lettuce and watercress soup 93
   pumpkin and ricotta soup with sautéed mushrooms 187
   roasted carrot and parsnip soup 146
spaghetti con fave e pecorino 27
spinach/spinachi 100
   cheesy spinach "terrine" 105
   spinach gnocchi 102
   spinach lasagne 101
strudel di verza con ricotta al forno 41
sweet and sour red cabbage 219
sweet potatoes 172
   sweet potato and chocolate loaf cake 174
Swiss chard 118
   filled flatbread from Emilia Romagna 124
   sweet chard tart 120

tarts
   arugula tart 90
   savory asparagus tart 20
   sweet chard tart 120
tomatoes 128–129
   arugula tart 90
   baked caprese "salad" 134
   celery pasta salad 49
   eggplant pasta bake 200–201
   eggplant "pizzette" 204
   eggplant "steaks" 203
   filled peppers 113

green beans with tomatoes 70
Italian-style baked potatoes 183
pea polpette served with a spicy tomato sauce 82
polenta lasagne with mushrooms 163–164
potato bake with tomatoes and capers 173
puntarelle and bread salad 95
quick tomato sauce 130
spinach gnocchi 102
stewed peppers 110
stuffed cabbage leaves in tomato sauce 38
stuffed tomatoes 133
tomato sorbet 136
traditional eggplant parmigiana 198–199
torta di carote e mandorle 148
torta di patata dolce e cioccolato 174
torta dolce di bietole 120
torta dolce di zucchine 61
torta salata di asparagi 20
torta salata di cipolle 170
torta salata di rucola 90
tortino di piselli 85
trofie con le puntarelle 96
tuna-filled artichoke hearts 11
turkey: stuffed cabbage leaves in tomato sauce 38

vellutata di broccoli con formaggio 31
vellutata di finocchi 64
vellutata di lattuga e crescione 93

walnuts
  celery pesto 44
  pasta with radicchio and creamy Gorgonzola 215
  sweet chard tart 120
watercress
  lettuce and watercress soup 93
  warm pumpkin salad 190
wine: broccoli cooked in red wine with provolone cheese 34

ziti pasta with onions 168
zucca 184–185
zucchine 50–51
zucchine fritte di Antonella 53
zucchine ripiene 55
zucchinis 50–51
  Antonella's fried zucchinis 53
  zucchini cake 61
  zucchini saltimbocca 54
  filled zucchini flowers 58
  filled zucchinis 55
  filled peppers 113
zuppa di porri e cannellini 75
zuppa di zucca e ricotta con funghi saltati 187

Grazie mille to all the lovely people who helped put this book together.

Liz Przybylski, for writing, recipe testing, and organizing

Adriana Contaldo, for recipe testing and cooking at the shoots.

David Loftus, for the wonderful photos throughout and such good company.

Pip Spence, for beautiful food and prop styling on set—and for spoiling us all with delicious treats while shooting!

Elisabetta Iudica, for wonderful illustrations.

My agent, Luigi Bonomi, for making this happen!

With thanks to the fabulous team at Pavilion Books for all their hard work and help at each stage of the process to make this book look stunning:

Stephanie Milner, for unwavering support.

Laura Russell, for all her design work and good times on shoots.

Ellen Simmons, for guiding us throughout the whole process and fun shoot days together.

Komal Patel, for finally coming to one of the shoots—your dish-washing and company was most appreciated!

First published in 2024 by

INTERLINK BOOKS
An imprint of Interlink Publishing Group, Inc.
46 Crosby Street
Northampton, Massachusetts 01060
www.interlinkbooks.com

Published simultaneously in Great Britain by Pavilion, an imprint of HarperCollinsPublishers Ltd.

Text © Gennaro Contaldo 2024

All rights reserved. No part of this work may be reproduced or utilized in any form or by any means, electronic or mechanical, including photocopying, recording, or by any information storage and retrieval system, without the prior written permission of the publisher.

Library of Congress Cataloging-in-Publication Data available
ISBN 978-1-62371-119-1

Printed and bound in Malaysia by COS/Papercraft
10 9 8 7 6 5 4 3 2 1

Publishing Director: Stephanie Milner
Editor: Ellen Simmons
American Edition Editor: Leyla Moushabeck
Design Director: Laura Russell
Designer: James Boast
American Edition Cover Design: Harrison Williams
Copyeditor: Vicki Murrell
Proofreaders: Anne Sheasby, Jane Bugaeva
Production Controller: Grace O'Byrne

This book is produced from independently certified FSC™ paper to ensure responsible forest management.

When using kitchen appliances please always follow the manufacturer's instructions.